SCIENTIFIC AMERICAN EXPLORES BIG IDEAS

Earth's Untouched Places

The Editors of *Scientific American*

SCIENTIFIC AMERICAN | EDUCATIONAL PUBLISHING
New York

Published in 2027 by Scientific American Educational Publishing
in association with **The Rosen Publishing Group**
2544 Clinton Street, Buffalo NY 14224

Contains material from Scientific American®, a division of Springer Nature America, Inc., reprinted by permission, as well as original material from The Rosen Publishing Group®.

First Edition

Scientific American
Lisa Pallatroni: Project Editor

Rosen Publishing
Nicole Horning: Compiling Editor
Michael Moy: Senior Graphic Designer

Cataloging-in-Publication Data
Names: Scientific American, Inc.
Title: Earth's untouched places / edited by the Scientific American Editors.
Description: Buffalo, New York : Scientific American Educational Publishing, an imprint of Rosen Publishing, 2027. | Series: Scientific American explores big ideas | Includes glossary and index.
Identifiers: ISBN 9781538314647 (pbk.) | ISBN 9781538314654 (library bound) | ISBN 9781538314661 (ebook)
Subjects: LCSH: Underwater exploration–Juvenile literature. | Arctic regions–Juvenile literature. | Amazon River region–Juvenile literature. | Climatic changes–Juvenile literature. | Environmental responsibility–Juvenile literature.
Classification: LCC GC65.E378 2027 | DDC 551.46–dc23

Manufactured in the United States of America
Websites listed were live at the time of publication.

Cover: golaminnovation/Shutterstock.com

CPSIA Compliance Information: Batch # CS27SA.
For Further Information contact Rosen Publishing at 1-800-237-9932.

CONTENTS

Introduction 6

Section 1: Under the Sea 7

1.1 We've Only Seen 0.001 Percent of Earth's Seafloor. Here's What That Really Means 8
By Gayoung Lee

1.2 Mining the Deep Sea Could Threaten a Source of Ocean Oxygen 12
By Rachel Feltman, Jeffery DelViscio, and Alex Sugiura

1.3 Stunning Antarctic Sea Creatures Discovered after Iceberg Breaks Away 22
By Ashley Balzer Vigil

1.4 Dive into a Vanishing Invisible Forest to See What Climate Has Changed 25
By Dominic Smith & Andrew Robinson

1.5 "Dark Oxygen" Discovered Coming from Mineral Deposits on Deep Seafloor 30
By Allison Parshall

1.6 Strange Ecosystem Found Thriving below Seafloor Hydrothermal Vents 34
By Jack Tamisiea

1.7 Ocean Discoveries Are Revising Long-Held Truths about Life 38
By Timothy Shank

1.8 Bizarro Life-Forms Inhabiting Deep-Sea Vents May Be at Risk 42
By Shannon Hall

1.9 Mysterious Galápagos Reefs Harbor Strawberry Squid and Other Fantastic Creatures 46
By Jack Tamisiea

1.10 Seals Show Scientists an Unknown Antarctic Canyon 49
By Ethan Freedman

1.11 The Ocean's Wilderness Areas Are Smaller Than You Think—and They're Disappearing Fast 51
By Kendall Jones & James Watson

1.12 Four New Octopus Species Discovered in the Deep Sea 54
By Ashley Balzer Vigil

1.13 The Mystery of Milky Seas Is Finally Being Solved 57
By Michelle Nijhuis

1.14 Bizarre Ecosystem Discovered More Than Two Miles beneath Arctic Ocean 67
By Claire Cameron

1.15 See the Lush Kelp Forests Scientists Are Fighting for as Oceans Warm 69
By Avery Schuyler Nunn

1.16 Science in Depth--Mini Subs Unlock Mysteries Deep Below the Ocean's Surface 71
By Emily Anthes

Section 2: Indigenous Lands 73

2.1 Indigenous Lands Ace Biodiversity Measurements 74
By Jason G. Goldman

2.2 Indigenous Amazon Communities Fight Deforestation with New Early-Alert Tool 76
By Annie Sneed

2.3 Great Nicobar Island Is a Paradise in Danger 78
By Madhusree Mukerjee

Section 3: The Arctic 93

3.1 Arctic Exploitation May Harm Animals Large and Small 94
By Chiara Eisner

3.2 The Arctic Is in Dire Straits, 20 Years of Reporting Show 99
By Andrea Thompson

Section 4: The Unknown 102

4.1 Out of Sight, 'Dark Fungi' Run the World from the Shadows 103
By Cody Cottier

4.2 Drones Sample Rare Specimens from Cliffs and Other Dangerous Places 108
By Susan Cosier

4.3 Under Soil and above Caves, a Warren of Hidden Life 111
By Jennifer Frazer

4.4 Volcano Erupts after Lying Dormant for 12,000 Years, Sending Scientists Scrambling 116
By Stephanie Pappas

4.5 Giant Volcano Rewrites the Story of Seafloor Formation 118
By William W. Sager

4.6 Meet the Magnificent Microbes of the Deep Unknown 123
By Jeffery DelViscio

4.7 Mangrove Trees Are on the Move, Taking the Tropics with Them 130
By Michael Adno

Section 5: How Climate Change is Impacting Untouched Places 140

5.1 How Climate Change Is Leaving Some Species with "Nowhere Left to Go" 141
By Fionna M. D. Samuels

5.2 The Reason Antarctica Is Melting: Shifting Winds, Driven by Global Warming 146
By Annie Sneed

5.3 Humans Have Crossed 7 of 9 "Planetary Boundaries" 150
By Andrea Thompson

Glossary 154

Further Information 156

Citations 158

Index 159

INTRODUCTION

The land, the sea, the sky...how big is it all, anyway? Have we seen everything there is to see? Are there undiscovered animals and plants out there? There are plenty of undiscovered things in the universe, whether hidden in remote jungles, in the sea, or in space. It's hard to know what we don't know, but we can have ideas about what's out there. The problem is, once something is found, it's no longer untouched. And human impacts such as global warming, deforestation, and other exploration activities can alter the discovered plant or animal, sometimes taking away its habitat.

This book is a collection of articles that explore some of these remarkable places that have remained untouched, while also looking at the impacts exploration activities can have on newly discovered areas, plants, and animals.

First, this book dives into an area that can be difficult to explore in "Under the Sea." You'll learn about new species, how much of the seafloor we've really seen, mysterious reefs, and more. From there, you'll discover regions cared for and lived in by Indigenous communities, whose knowledge and traditions have preserved these environments over time. Then, you'll explore the Arctic, one of the most extreme and rapidly changing places on Earth. "The Unknown" takes you even further into places and things scientists are still trying to understand.

In the last chapter, you'll explore the effects of what happens when places, animals, and plants aren't as untouched as they once were and how climate change is impacting even the most remote parts of the world. Rising temperatures, melting ice, and shifting ecosystems remind us that no place is completely isolated from the consequences of human impact, and that protecting these places and things are vital to the future of life on Earth.

Section 1: Under the Sea

1.1 We've Only Seen 0.001 Percent of Earth's Seafloor. Here's What That Really Means
By Gayoung Lee

1.2 Mining the Deep Sea Could Threaten a Source of Ocean Oxygen
By Rachel Feltman, Jeffery DelViscio & Alex Sugiura

1.3 Stunning Antarctic Sea Creatures Discovered after Iceberg Breaks Away
By Ashley Balzer Vigil

1.4 Dive into a Vanishing Invisible Forest to See What Climate Has Changed
By Dominic Smith & Andrew Robinson

1.5 "Dark Oxygen" Discovered Coming from Mineral Deposits on Deep Seafloor
By Allison Parshall

1.6 Strange Ecosystem Found Thriving below Seafloor Hydrothermal Vents
By Jack Tamisiea

1.7 Ocean Discoveries Are Revising Long-Held Truths about Life
By Timothy Shank

1.8 Bizarro Life-Forms Inhabiting Deep-Sea Vents May Be at Risk
By Shannon Hall

1.9 Mysterious Galápagos Reefs Harbor Strawberry Squid and Other Fantastic Creatures
By Jack Tamisiea

1.10 Seals Show Scientists an Unknown Antarctic Canyon
By Ethan Freedman

1.11 The Ocean's Wilderness Areas Are Smaller Than You Think—and They're Disappearing Fast
By Kendall Jones & James Watson

1.12 Four New Octopus Species Discovered in the Deep Sea
By Ashley Balzer Vigil

1.13 The Mystery of Milky Seas Is Finally Being Solved
By Michelle Nijhuis

1.14 Bizarre Ecosystem Discovered More Than Two Miles beneath Arctic Ocean
By Claire Cameron

1.15 See the Lush Kelp Forests Scientists Are Fighting for as Oceans Warm
By Avery Schuyler Nunn

1.16 Slide Show: Science in Depth--Mini Subs Unlock Mysteries Deep Below the Ocean's Surface
By Emily Anthes

We've Only Seen 0.001 Percent of Earth's Seafloor. Here's What That Really Means

By Gayoung Lee

What do we *really* know about the deep ocean? Whether Earth's ocean is an ecological paradise teeming with wildlife or a mysterious, stormy underworld hiding mythological sea monsters, it goes without saying that our ignorance of the aqueous abyss has shaped our perception of what could exist there. But in terms of actually tallying up what we *do* know about the deep seafloor, establishing certainty has been elusive.

"In scientific papers, some people [said] we've explored 5 percent or 10 percent or 1 percent [of the deep ocean]–and there was no consensus," says Katy Croff Bell, a marine scientist and founder of the Ocean Discovery League. She wondered "Has anybody actually calculated this?" Bell adds. "And I couldn't find anything. So I started to do just initial estimates about four or five years ago, and the numbers seemed ridiculously small: 0.001 percent [visited and explored] over almost [the past] 70 years."

That couldn't be right, Bell remembers thinking. But follow-up investigations confirmed her suspicions that we humans indeed had only directly observed less than 0.001 percent of the global seafloor–a total area that is about the same as that of Rhode Island. That's a shockingly tiny amount, considering we've now managed to obtain high-resolution images of practically all of the surfaces of the moon and Mars.

As detailed in a study published on May 7 in *Science Advances*, Bell and her co-authors compared 43,681 records from submersible expeditions that were conducted by institutions in by 14 countries and territories and had each reached a minimum of 200 meters (about 656 feet) beneath the waves. In addition to our generally limited understanding of the global seafloor, Bell and her colleagues also found a significant bias in the regions that did have visual reconnaissance. Unsurprisingly, most direct observations of the deep sea occurred in the waters around wealthy countries with the capability to conduct them–especially the U.S., Japan and New Zealand.

But what does Bell's "0.001 percent" figure really mean? Do we truly know less of the seafloor than we do of the moon or Mars? The correct answer, according to researchers, is no, although this pushback comes with important caveats. For one, it's worth noting that the 99.999 percent statistic explicitly represents what we have not "directly seen" of the deep seafloor–meaning all that we have not surveyed via visual imaging. This is different from mapping, which can measure seafloor topography with or without visual data collection. "Seeing" is also not the same as "sampling," the gathering of geological or biological specimens from a particular area. These three elements–visual imaging, terrain mapping and physical sampling–constitute fully "exploring" an unknown environment, Bell says.

With that in mind, it's not so shocking that Bell's number would be so small, says Alfred McEwen, principal investigator for the High Resolution Imaging Experiment on NASA's Mars Reconnaissance Orbiter and a planetary geologist at the University of Arizona, who was not involved in the new work. Orbital surveillance has indeed allowed us to create stunningly detailed visual maps of the surface of the moon and Mars that far exceed those we have for Earth's ocean floor. But that's different from *understanding*, McEwen says. "I mean, you can map the topography and the brightness and color variations and have nice-looking maps," he adds. "But that doesn't mean you understand what's there in terms of composition, relevant processes, and so on."

Additionally, any talk of directly observing Earth's seafloor versus the surfaces of Mars and the moon "is a little bit of an apples-to-oranges comparison," says Mathieu Lapôtre, a geophysicist at Stanford University, who was also not involved in the study. The former is hidden beneath kilometers of cold, dark, crushingly pressurized water, while the latter can be seen clearly from a spacecraft passing far overhead.

But we've managed to come up with very clever ways to unveil the ocean's depths, Lapôtre says. For example, using altimeters on satellites or sonar technology, it's more than possible to build a pretty accurate model of what the bottom of the sea looks like. In that sense, there's probably more we "understand" about the ocean floor—particularly regarding its role in shaping Earth systems—than we do about the surface of the moon or Mars, McEwen says. And at least partially by virtue of our proximity and familiarity with the ocean and all its complexities, he adds, it seems to us a richer, more vibrant place, with "dynamically changing environments, undersea vents, and so forth—there's a lot more to understand on Earth."

Even if we do, in fact, "know" Earth's oceans better than the surface of any otherworldly body, that doesn't mean we know everything or that there are no benefits to higher-resolution optical data of the deep sea, says Brett Denevi, a planetary scientist at Johns Hopkins Applied Physics Laboratory, who is involved with NASA's Lunar Reconnaissance Orbiter and was not a part of the new work. As our maps of the moon have improved, Denevi explains, we have not solved all lunar mysteries but instead revealed new ones. The more we learn, the more we see, the better, it seems, that we can pinpoint smaller, more subtle environmental details that coarser-grained mapping or sampling might otherwise miss.

"And often, the smaller things might be the important things, right?" Lapôtre says. "The ocean bottom, we know, is very complex. It has all these features that are fascinating for many reasons—for example, the origins of life, plate tectonics, and the subduction zones and all those things—it's a complex terrain. And right now we're missing a lot of that complexity."

"Imagine owning a house but never going down to the basement to figure out how your heater or electrical system works," Bell says. For example, she says, it was only in the 1970s that humanity found out about thriving ecosystems around hydrothermal vents—a discovery that showed biology could flourish even in the ocean's sunless depths and "changed our understanding of life on Earth." Indirect mapping from sonar and other techniques allows you to "see" the mid-ocean ridges that host some of these vents. But actually finding the vents was a serendipitous discovery that was only made possible by deep-sea cameras.

And, Bell points out, given the wonders we've already witnessed by our direct visitations of just 0.001 percent of the seafloor, the prospects for further revolutionary observations are good. The abysmally low figure for our visual knowledge of the abyss is cause for excitement, not dismay, she says. Paired with burgeoning technological advances to make submarine exploration better, cheaper and safer, Bell's assessment is an invitation to begin "an unbiased and more representative look at the global deep seafloor."

"On the exploration side of things, the [new study] really lays the groundwork for setting out a global initiative that we should undertake in the next 10 to 20 years," Bell says. "Being able to explore, or at least accelerate, the exploration of the other 99.999 percent of the deep ocean is really going to give us an amazing opportunity to ask new questions we'd never even thought of before."

About the Author

Gayoung Lee is a science journalist and former news intern and Games ace at Scientific American. *A philosopher turned journalist, originally from South Korea, Lee is interested finding unexpected connections between life and different science, particularly in theoretical physics and mathematics. You can read more about her here: https://gayoung-lee.carrd.co*

Mining the Deep Sea Could Threaten a Source of Ocean Oxygen

By Rachel Feltman, Jeffery DelViscio, and Alex Sugiura

Rachel Feltman: For *Scientific American's Science Quickly*, I'm Rachel Feltman.

Scattered across the deep ocean floor are trillions of potato-sized black rocks packed with valuable metals such cobalt and copper. Mining companies want to harvest these nodules to get materials for electric vehicle batteries and other clean energy tech. But recent research suggests the rocks might be producing oxygen in the darkness of the deep sea—potentially supporting marine life in ways we're just beginning to understand.

Today we're joined by Clare Fieseler and Jason Jaacks, who recently explored these mysterious deep-sea rocks in a mini documentary for *Scientific American*. Jason is a documentary filmmaker and an associate professor of journalism at the University of Rhode Island, and Clare is a scientist as well as a journalist for Canary Media, a nonprofit news outlet focused on clean energy and climate change.

Thank you both so much for coming on to chat.
Clare Fieseler: Thanks for having us.
Jason Jaacks: Yeah, thank you.

Feltman: So let's start with a, a basic question: What are nodules, and how do scientists think that they're formed?

Fieseler: Nodules look like little black potato-sized rocks, and they cover these vast areas of the abyssal plain, the bottom of the ocean. They contain significant amounts of critical minerals like manganese and copper and cobalt, and we didn't even know about them until the 1870s, when the HMS *Challenger*, which was the world's first oceanographic expedition, went out and dragged up a bunch of stuff from the deep sea in the Pacific, and these black rocks tumbled onto the deck of the ship, and they're like, "Oh, what are these?"

At first they were just on display in Victorian museums like moon rocks, and then in, like, the 1950s and '60s scientists started to kind of realize that–or at least they hypothesized–that these had been formed over millions and millions of years, that they likely started off as little, tiny bits of what they call anuclei, and it's, like, a shark tooth or a whale ear bone or a piece of pumice from, from an exploded volcano. Parts of debris fall to the ocean floor, and then through a process called sorption, they begin to almost accumulate minerals from the seawater in these layers. And actually, when you can cut into one you'll see these rings that look like tree rings, and you can age a nodule by counting those rings.

And so they're infinitely fascinating from a scientific perspective, and now they're also fascinating from an economic perspective, which we'll probably talk about.

Feltman: Definitely gonna get into that. But like you said these aren't really much to look at at first glance, but they can apparently upend our understanding of how life started on Earth. How is that?

Jaacks: One of the remarkable things about these nodules is that they provide habitat for all kinds of different creatures, and those are creatures that we can see, but they also provide habitat for all kinds of interesting microbial life.

You know, some of these nodules, they have a really kind of rough exterior; there's a lot of little kind of nooks and crannies in there. And so one of our sources described those nodules to us as a "Manhattan ..."

Feltman: Mm.

Jaacks: "For microbes": you know, there's different neighborhoods; there's different kind of places for all of these different microbes to, to live within the nodules themselves.

How that might change our understanding about how life began on Earth was that there was a study that came out last year that looked at the production of oxygen–that these nodules were actually producing oxygen within a chamber. They basically noticed that oxygen levels within this chamber were going up. So if that is, in fact, correct, then the rocks themselves were producing oxygen.

Fieseler: And at first they thought it could be this world of microbes that live within the nodule–maybe *they* are producing the oxygen, right, not the rock itself. And that might still be the case, but the source we interviewed for this film, Dr. Jeff Marlow, put in kind of like this chemical cocktail that acts as a poison to kill those microbes, and after they introduced that to their experiment the nodules were *still* producing oxygen from in that chamber.

And so if they successfully killed all the microbes that were living in that nodule, then it must be something else. It might be the rock itself, right? And so the paper is very preliminary and exploratory, and the scientists even admit, like, "We need to do a lot more studies, but we think it's not the microbes; we think it's actually the rock itself."

Feltman: Wow.

Fieseler: How do rocks produce oxygen at the bottom of the sea in complete darkness, without the presence of photosynthesis? Like, this is the mind-blowing side of things. The scientists are still trying to understand what that process is, but they think it's something called seawater electrolysis: essentially where the nodule is acting like a battery to power a process that produces this oxygen. And we know that that exists, but whether it's happening here is still being investigated.

So yeah, batteries at the bottom of the sea is the key takeaway there.

Feltman: Wow, I mean, even just "Manhattan for microbes" is so evocative, and then the oxygen stuff is, like, almost a little spooky in a very cool way [laughs]. But as Clare alluded to earlier there are other reasons to care about these nodules. What about the, the economic interest in these nodules? Where's that coming from?

Fieseler: These nodules contain minerals that are absolutely essential for electric vehicle batteries that are made today. This week I bought a Kia EV9, which is an electric vehicle, and in my new car, in the giant battery underneath my feet as I drive, there's enough cobalt where you want a [reliable] supply chain of cobalt if you want kind of a clean-car revolution for the United States and for the world. And cobalt exists in high quantities in these nodules, and cobalt doesn't really exist in these dense amounts in other places; it's not as common. We get most of our cobalt from the Democratic Republic of the Congo, which has its own issues with human rights abuses and so forth.

And so there are people who've long thought, "Well, this seems like a better way, from a human-rights perspective, to get our cobalt for a green revolution." But I think there's also, like–it's definitely a problematic narrative [laughs].

Feltman: Mm.

Fieseler: And we can talk about that later.

Feltman: Yeah, well, that's actually–it's a great segue. My next question was just gonna be: you know, you guys made a film about the nodules, so I would love to hear more about what tensions exist around them and, and who the players are in this conversation.

Jaacks: Yeah, so in making this film we discovered this kind of core tension between trying to understand this environment, this place that we really don't know much about, and these little potato-sized kind of alien rocks from the bottom of the sea it turns out have this, you know, economic potential that we didn't really know about prior. So especially as we try to electrify our economy these are really valuable minerals.

So the tension that we really were exploring in the film was: How do we understand these nodules? You know, in one way they are the substrate and they provide this structure for life at the bottom of the sea, and do we want to try to understand that, or do we use those resources kind of in the short term to electrify our economies so that we can avert some of the worst impacts of, of climate change?

So that tension between: What are these rocks for? Do they have, you know, value laying on the seafloor because they might be potentially producing oxygen or because they provide this entire habitat for what is, ultimately, the default habitat on Earth? I mean, the abyssal plains covers [about] 60 percent of, of the surface area of Earth if you were to lift the oceans; this is an immense habitat. So do the nodules have a place in that, or do they belong in batteries in, in our vehicles?

And so we interview a number of scientists who are interested as part of their research in studying the deep, but we also look at the evolution of the value of nodules kind of economically. And Clare stumbled across this incredible story that actually led to the rediscovery of the very first deep-sea mining site, which happened off the coast of South Carolina.

Fieseler: You might be hearing about deep-sea mining for the first time now—deep-sea mining has been around for about 50 years. It was Americans that kind of invented it.

In the 19—or late 1960s very wealthy individuals, I call them the 1960s version of Silicon bros, you know, they were just like, "Let's do crazy stuff." You know, "We just put a man on the moon; let's go dig up minerals from the bottom of the sea."

And so a wealthy shipbuilder poured a bunch of money into this endeavor, and in 1970 they tested it successfully over 100 miles off the coast of South Carolina. But then, you know, it never was really economically profitable. The technology was cool, you know, they wanted to prove that they could do it, but yet a lot of these early deep-sea mining companies went bankrupt because the economics were never there.

But what was so interesting is that they left this legacy of experimentation on the bottom of the seafloor. And one of the characters in our film, Dr. Jason Chaytor, he kind of stumbled upon mention of the world's first deep-sea mining experiment site, which had been completely lost by the U.S. government. It only existed in, like, handwritten notes in a storage facility in Woods Hole, Massachusetts, that he took us to.

And he spent years trying to, like, piece together what happened and where it was, and he got money from the U.S. government to go back to just see, like, "What does this place look like [more than] 50 years later?" They didn't know what they were gonna see. And the very first time I spoke to him about this, I said, "Well, what did it look like when you brought robots, you know, to the bottom of the sea [more than] 50 years after mining?" He said, "It looked like they were there yesterday."

That really kind of, like, gave me goose bumps, and I knew I kind of wanted to pursue this further. So I told Jason, who is a longtime friend of mine, I was like, "This story's crazy. This history's crazy. No one really knows about it, and the government lost track of it. Like, let's start following this." And that's kind of how this film came to be.

Feltman: Very cool. I would love to hear more about the study that the Metals Company paid for that they're now contesting the results of. What, what happened there?

Fieseler: So the Metals Company, in pursuit of a license to extract minerals in an area beyond national jurisdiction, which just means, like, an area of the ocean that doesn't belong to any country–it's, it's the high seas, right?

Feltman: Mm-hmm.

Fieseler: And technically, under a global treaty that most of the world's countries have signed, that area is designated under international law as the "common heritage" of all mankind: the [more than] eight billion people alive today and all future generations to come.

So that deep-sea area, it belongs to everybody, and so in order to get a license to exploit it *all* the countries that have signed on to this treaty need to kind of agree on how that's gonna happen, how they're gonna do that. And countries haven't yet agreed on how to do that–they're, they're very close.

And so in preparation for getting approval, in theory, this company got [exploration permits], so they're kind of doing the, the studies, and they had to pay scientists to kind of understand what's down there, right? "If we go and mine this area with the approval of all these countries under this treaty called the Law of the Sea, we need to make sure that it's gonna have–you know, understand our impact down there." They had to pay for this science, and this discovery of oxygen production was *completely unexpected*, and it just happens that the results are just not great for the company's sales pitch.

Feltman: Mm-hmm.

Fieseler: The sales pitch is that this is a "marine desert"; there's no life down there. These rocks, they're just kind of sitting out there like golf balls on a fairway–scoop 'em up and no harm, no foul, right? If that's not the case, as this science is suggesting, if they're producing oxygen then, you know, removing them, it is, like, way more risky than we thought.

The day that the paper came out it created a lot of hubbub, a lot of news coverage, and also a lot of the delegates who were meeting at that very moment of the countries that have all signed the Law of the Sea, they were talking about the potential of deep-sea mining, they started bringing up this new study. And almost right away the Metals Company, who had funded the research, started trying to discredit it.

Feltman: Mm.

Fieseler: There's a rebuttal online that people can go and find–if you look at the Metals Company "dark oxygen" rebuttal–but it's worth mentioning that there's a peer-review process here, right?

Feltman: Sure.

Fieseler: If you're refuting a peer-reviewed study, then you have to submit your arguments and your rebuttal to the peer-reviewed journal where it was published. And so the Metals Company is in the process of doing that, but the rebuttal has not yet passed peer review.

Feltman: Hmm.

Fieseler: Right? So it has not kind of gotten the stamp of approval from other peers that their *rebuttal* has scientific merit.

Feltman: How might we expect the story about these nodules to evolve in the coming months?

Fieseler: There [are] a couple things happening. At first the researchers of the "dark oxygen" study, they *lost* their funding because their funding was coming from the Metals Company. But Andrew Sweetman, who was the lead co-author of the study, he actually got quite a bit of money to continue research on this. So research on "dark oxygen" is moving forward; that's one thing.

We're waiting to see if the rebuttal passes peer review, what that looks like. But, you know, there's a new player in this space, and that is the Trump administration. The Trump administration has put out an executive order to essentially support companies to mine the deep sea in areas outside of U.S. waters, and this is really controversial.

Jaacks: So the International Seabed Authority, they're this international body that is designated to regulate how mining companies will move forward. We were just at their 30th meeting in Kingston, Jamaica, where their organization is headquartered, for the assembly in which all the delegates from the countries that have signed on, they were all there to continue this global conversation about how to move forward or whether to move forward.

They didn't come to a conclusion at the end of this meeting; they meet twice a year. There's also this tension between an administration that is trying to move unilaterally and move in a different direction than a global organization that was specifically established to regulate and come up with rules about how we might exploit these kinds of resources. So, you know, there's going to be this continuing battle between the American position on deep-sea mining and a global one, so we'll continue to watch that as it develops.

Feltman: Absolutely. Thank you both so much for coming on to talk us through this. It's been great.

Fieseler: Thanks for having us.

Jaacks: Thank you so much for having us, yeah. Appreciate it.

Feltman: That's all for today's episode. For more on these mysterious nodules, check out Clare and Jason's documentary about the subject over on *Scientific American*'s YouTube channel. You can find a link to that in our show notes.

About the Authors

Rachel Feltman is former executive editor of Popular Science *and forever host of the podcast* The Weirdest Thing I Learned This Week. *She previously founded the blog Speaking of Science for the Washington Post.*

Jeffery DelViscio is currently chief multimedia editor/executive producer at Scientific American. *He is former director of multimedia at* STAT, *where he oversaw all visual, audio and interactive journalism. Before that he spent more than eight years at the New York Times, where he worked on five different desks across the paper. He holds dual master's degrees in journalism and in Earth and environmental sciences from Columbia University. He has worked onboard oceanographic research vessels and tracked money and politics in science from Washington, D.C. He was a Knight Science Journalism Fellow at the Massachusetts Institute of Technology in 2018. His work has won numerous awards, including two News and Documentary Emmy Awards.*

Alex Sugiura is a Peabody and Pulitzer Prize–winning composer, editor and podcast producer based in Brooklyn, N.Y. He has worked on projects for Bloomberg, Axios, Crooked Media *and Spotify, among others.*

Stunning Antarctic Sea Creatures Discovered after Iceberg Breaks Away

By Ashley Balzer Vigil

In H. P. Lovecraft's chilling science-fiction novella *At the Mountains of Madness*, a group of researchers uncovers the ruins of an ancient alien civilization while exploring beneath Antarctica. Now a real team has investigated what lies beneath some of the frozen continent's floating ice, and its findings are certainly otherworldly.

Scientists onboard the Schmidt Ocean Institute's research vessel *Falkor (too)* sailed to Antarctica to study the nearby seafloor, the creatures that live there and the way climate change is affecting Antarctic ice and the ecosystems that evolved around it. But their plan was sidetracked after an iceberg the size of Chicago broke away from a nearby ice shelf in Bellingshausen Sea on January 13.

That event presented an opportunity that was too good to pass up: the chance to explore the seafloor below the iceberg's original location–like overturning a rock or log in the woods to see what creatures lie hidden underneath. "There was a sense of going into a complete unknown," says the expedition's co-chief scientist Sasha Montelli of University College London. "We thought we might see some life there, but it was really surprising to see the degree to which life was thriving in such a hostile environment. And it wasn't just existing there but had apparently been sustained for a very long time."

The researchers sent their underwater robot *SuBastian* into the deep and found an ecosystem filled with anemones that look like Dr. Seuss's Truffula Trees, along with sea spiders, icefish and octopuses. Some of the creatures are new species, and many may only be found near Antarctica. Beyond simply being remote, the continent has been isolated for millions of years by the Antarctic Circumpolar Current, which surrounds it like a moat around a castle.

"Because the Bellingshausen Sea is not much explored in terms of deep-sea biodiversity, we expect many new species from the expedition. And in fact, we have already confirmed some, including snails, polychaete worms, crustaceans and even fish," says the expedition's co-chief scientist Patricia Esquete of the Center for Environmental and Marine Studies and the University of Aveiro in Portugal.

The researchers also encountered large vaselike sponges whose size hints at their age. "Based on the size of the animals, the communities we observed have been there for decades, maybe even hundreds of years," Esquete said in a recent press release.

The observations draw sharp contrast to previous studies of ecology below the ice, which either dropped cameras down through holes drilled in the ice or took place years after an iceberg calved. "Those studies indicated that the ecosystems seemed to be quite impoverished, with a limited number of species," Esquete says. "Now we know that under ice shelves, at least in the first 15 kilometers from the front"--the newly exposed area the new expedition's researchers were able to explore after the iceberg calved--"there are diverse, well-established ecosystems."

Less certain is how this vibrant ecosystem will fare now that the iceberg has broken away. Many deep-sea dwellers are adapted to unchanging conditions found in their environment, so they are highly sensitive to even small environmental shifts. For the life-forms uncovered in Bellingshausen Sea, the dramatic loss of their former iceberg ceiling may rock their ecosystem.

Montelli says that the floating ice shelf that the iceberg broke away from has retreated inland by about 25 miles (40 km) over the past 50 years–just one example of accelerating ice loss on the continent. "The ice loss from the Antarctic Ice Sheet is a major contributor to sea level rise worldwide," Montelli said in the recent press release. "Our work is critical for providing longer-term context of these recent changes, improving our ability to make projections of future change."

About the Author

Ashley Balzer Vigil writes about astrophysics for NASA's Goddard Space Flight Center by day and moonlights as a freelance environmental writer.

Dive into a Vanishing Invisible Forest to See What Climate Has Changed

By Dominic Smith & Andrew Robinson

Josh Smith: I started initially studying terrestrial ecology, but I stumbled into a scuba diving class where I learned to dive right here along the Monterey breakwater wall. It was a really rough day. The surf was big. We barely made it into the water. And I mean, we couldn't even hardly see our hands in front of our faces because it was so murky. It's freezing cold. And I just thought it was the coolest thing. I was like, it can't get better than this.

And from that moment, I just became fascinated by kelp forest ecosystems.

My name is Josh Smith, and I am a postdoctoral researcher at the National Center for Ecological Analysis and Synthesis. I've been studying kelp forest ecology for about 11 years.

Most of my research has been specifically in Monterey Bay. Being in a kelp forest is much like being in a redwood forest.

Kelp grow really tall. They grow all the way from the sea floor up to the surface. They can grow up to 80 feet tall. The reef is covered in life of all kinds of different colors, invertebrates and fishes that are on the bottom underwater. There's life everywhere, all the way up to the surface.

Pete Raimondi: We set up surveys years and years ago. They started in 1992 and it was in response to the Exxon Valdez oil spill, which was up in Alaska. But there was this recognition that we knew very little about these habitats. And if we are going to be able to assess damages, you kind of needed to know what was there. And one of the things that affords, of course, is that you have the opportunity to see change. And you can see that there are these coastal ecosystems, kelp forests and rocky intertidal areas, and things come and go and they change.

My name is Pete Raimondi. I'm a professor at UC Santa Cruz in the Department of Ecology and Evolutionary Biology. My primary interest is in kelp forests along the coast of California and rocky intertidal areas, which we think of as tidepools.

Smith: Back when we were driving this area, 2012, 2013, the kelp was so thick that we'd have to anchor the boat way out here and then swim under the canopy to get to the location where we were going to do our surveys. Now we can pretty much just pull up right to our dive site, you know, drop anchor and go.

But in 2013, things began to seriously change.

Raimondi: It was shocking. I'd never seen anything like it. We saw starfish starting to disintegrate, basically in front of us. We would see these things on the bottom that we call Ghost Stars, which were the (white) outline of the sea star. The white was bacteria.

Smith: All these sea stars were basically just dissolving under water. They lose their arms, they twist and get torsion. And it's really pretty nasty.

Raimondi: It was like the underwater world was in its last stages.

Smith: That sea star wasting syndrome decimated several species of sea stars up and down the coast. One species that was hit particularly hard was this sunflower sea star that we call Pycnopodia. And this is a very large sea star that grows to be the size of an extra large pizza. They have 24 arms and they cruise along the reef for sea urchins.

And sea urchins are these spiny baseball sized animals that like to eat kelp. Now, normally in a kelp forest, these native sea urchin grazers are living down, tucked away in the cracks and crevices and they're eating drift kelp.

In 2014, we had a major marine heat wave. These marine heatwaves are a product of climate change, and all of these anomalies are like nothing we've seen, you know, in the last 100 years, one was the blob, which was this really warm seawater that showed up in the northeastern Pacific Ocean.

And the other was this warm equatorial water that came up that was from a major El Nino event. And so this major marine heat wave just completely bathed all of central and northern California. And this really warm water and kelp needs really cold, nutrient rich water to thrive.

Raimondi: And so the combination of lots and lots of sea urchins and very bad environmental conditions for kelp caused the kelp forests to collapse.

Smith: We're really hoping to learn more about sea urchin behavior. We want to know how much kelp sea urchins actually eat and what's that critical point when sea urchins shift from passively grazing on drift where they're tucked away in the crevices to now storming out of the crevices, eating live kelp. That's a really fundamentally important behavioral shift that we're really interested in learning more about.

These sea urchins in many places, completely clear cut the kelp all the way to the reef surface and formed what we call sea urchin barrens. And these are places where the urchins have overgrazed the kelp. There's no macroalgae left. It's just a carpet of purple.

We've discussed the sea urchins that eat kelp, and we discussed the Sunflower Sea Star, which is a known predator of sea urchins. There's another predator of sea urchins that we have here in Monterey Bay, and that's the Southern Sea Otter. Part of the reason why we still have patches of kelp forests along the Monterey Peninsula is because the otters are helping to maintain those remnant patches of kelp forests. They are targeting the healthy urchins in those patches of kelp. However, because the otters are not foraging on sea urchins in the barrens, they're not actively contributing to recovery.

These are the the major grazers that are eating all of the kelp. So these urchins, again, they emerged from crevices and they were no longer eating drift and they started eating live kelp. So in the lab, we're looking to see what actually causes that behavioral shift. How do predators play a part in that?

So it's been really remarkable to see how fast the ecosystem can change, how quickly kelp can become deforested, and how quickly these sea urchin barrens can happen. And I wish I could just look back into time and see how often does this happen before? How long did the Barrens persist? Were there barrens? Because to us, it seems like this happened really quickly. We lost all the kelp.

I have to remind myself that my perception and my window into these changing forest ecosystems is just a fraction of time on the geologic time scale.

Raimondi: The kelp forests seem to be recovering right now, and we're in a period of really cold water and at least recently and things seem to be coming back in.

We're in a pretty fortunate situation, to be completely honest, because I think that unlike a lot of environments, people actually are very interested in this. This interest has led to an immense amount of information that we would not have had. So like in the sea star wasting, probably 90 percent of the information that was from people, citizens, and that's because they're interested and they care.

And so I think that that's a huge plus, and I would just hope that that stays.

Smith: It's hard to speculate about what might happen. These are really dynamic ecosystems. There are all kinds of invertebrates and birds and things that depend on kelp as a subsidy.

The kelp also ends up offshore and in the canyon, and so the kelp that's ripped out eventually makes its way offshore. Some of it sinks down. It's not just important for the animals that live there, but kelp forests are also fundamentally important in buffering climate change. In one way that they do that is like plants on land kelp actually take in CO2.

And when that kelp is ripped out and transported offshore, that carbon that the kelp has has captured is ultimately sequestered into deep sea sediments.

Interviewer: And what's so great about kelp?
Smith: You're not convinced already?

Well, kelp is what we call a foundation species. So it supports the entire forest ecosystem by providing habitat and food for all of the animals that live here.

With all of these changes that are happening, what we're seeing is the foundation being unraveled. It's being deforested, and it's not being deforested because of harvest. It's being deforested because of these other processes that are happening, these marine heatwaves and the sea urchin outbreaks that can occur over several hundred kilometers with ocean warming globally and climate change, you know, like a blob that really initiated all of this back in 2014, that that blob was this area of warm water that showed up in the northeastern Pacific Ocean.

And my understanding still that, you know, we don't really know why it showed up. It just did. And it's unclear how kelp forests are going to respond to these recurring marine heatwaves.

About the Author

Dominic Smith is an Emmy winning multimedia producer, visual effects artist and journalist based in New Hampshire. He operates Smith Robinson Multimedia with offices in New England and California. Follow Dominic Smith on Twitter.

Andrew Robinson is a documentary producer, journalist, and writer living in Los Angeles, CA. His Emmy award winning production company, Smith Robinson Multimedia produces long and short form video focusing on science and the outdoors. Follow Andrew Robinson on Twitter.

"Dark Oxygen" Discovered Coming from Mineral Deposits on Deep Seafloor

By Allison Parshall

The dark seabed of the Pacific Ocean's Clarion-Clipperton Zone (CCZ) is littered with what look like hunks of charcoal. These unassuming metal deposits, called polymetallic nodules, contain metals such as manganese and cobalt used to produce batteries, marking them as targets for deep-sea mining companies.

Now researchers have discovered that the valuable nodules do something remarkable: they produce oxygen and do so without sunlight. "This is a totally new and unexpected finding," says Lisa Levin, an emeritus professor of biological oceanography at the Scripps Institution of Oceanography, who was not involved in the current research.

According to Boston University microbiologist Jeffrey Marlow, the idea that some of Earth's oxygen gas may come not from photosynthesizing organisms but from inanimate minerals in total darkness "really strongly goes against what we traditionally think of as where oxygen is made and how it's made." Marlow is a co-author of the new study, which was published in *Nature Geoscience*.

The story of discovery goes back to 2013, when deep-sea ecologist Andrew Sweetman was facing a frustrating problem. His team had been trying to measure how much oxygen organisms on the CCZ seafloor consumed. The researchers sent landers down more than 13,000 feet and created enclosed chambers on the seabed to track how oxygen levels in the water fell over time.

But oxygen levels did not fall. Instead they rose significantly. Thinking the sensors were broken, Sweetman sent the instruments back to the manufacturer. "This happened four or five times" over the course of five years, says Sweetman, who studies seafloor ecology and biogeochemistry at the Scottish Association for Marine Science. "I literally told my students, 'Throw the sensors in the bin. They just do not work.'"

Then, in 2021, he returned to the CCZ on a survey expedition sponsored by the Metals Company, a deep-sea mining firm. Again, his team used landers to make enclosed chambers on the seafloor and monitor oxygen levels. They used a different technique to measure oxygen this time but observed the same strange results: oxygen levels increased dramatically. "Suddenly, I realized that I'd been ignoring this hugely significant process, and I just kicked myself," Sweetman says.

The researchers initially thought deep-sea microbes were producing the oxygen. That idea once might have seemed far-fetched, but scientists had recently discovered that some microbes can generate "dark oxygen" in the absence of sunlight. In laboratory tests that reproduced conditions on the seafloor, Sweetman and his colleagues poisoned seawater with mercury chloride to kill off the microbes. Yet oxygen levels still increased.

If this dark oxygen didn't come from a biological process, then it must have come from a geological one, the scientists reasoned. They tested a few possible hypotheses–such as that radioactivity in the nodules was decomposing seawater molecules to make oxygen or that something was pulling oxygen from the nodules' manganese oxide–but ultimately ruled them out. Then, one day in 2022, Sweetman was watching a video about deep-sea mining when he heard the nodules referred to as "a battery in a rock." That bit of marketing was only a metaphor, but it led him to wonder whether the nodules could somehow be acting as natural geobatteries. If they were electrically charged, they could potentially split seawater into hydrogen and oxygen through a process called seawater electrolysis. (A battery dropped in salt water produces a similar effect.)

"Amazingly, there was almost a volt [of electric charge] on the surface of these nodules," Sweetman says; for comparison, an AA battery carries about 1.5 volts. The nodules may become charged as they grow, as different metals are deposited irregularly over the course of millions of years and a gradient of charge develops between each layer. Seawater electrolysis is currently the researchers' leading theory for dark oxygen production, and they plan to test it further.

It isn't clear, however, whether (or to what extent) these nodules create oxygen naturally on the seabed. In most experiments, oxygen production ceased after two days, which may indicate that the lander caused it by disrupting something about the environment. But it's also possible that the reaction eventually stopped because of a "bottle effect" within the enclosed chamber, Marlow says. "The products build up, the reactants go away, and then the reaction sort of stops. But in an open system ... it could be a more consistent process," he explains.

Bo Barker Jørgensen, a marine biogeochemist at the Max Planck Institute for Marine Microbiology in Bremen, Germany, is skeptical that these nodules produce oxygen when they are left undisturbed on the seabed. (Jørgensen was not involved in the research but was one of the paper's peer reviewers for *Nature Geoscience*.) Still, it does seem that the nodules are producing oxygen through electrolysis, he adds, "and that in itself is a very interesting observation that has not been observed before, to my knowledge."

The researchers don't yet know whether this oxygen would be important to life on the CCZ seabed. The nodules and surrounding sediment are a habitat for deep-sea life, from tiny microbes to larger "megafauna," such as fish and sea stars. Half of the ecosystem's megafauna is found only on the nodules. This is a "poorly understood ecosystem," Levin says. "We haven't even discovered most of the species in the deep sea, let alone studied them."

Proposed deep-sea mining projects would extract nodules from swaths of the CCZ seafloor. The International Seabed Authority (ISA) is still drafting rules and regulations for mining the nodules and other deep-sea targets. At least 32 member states of the ISA have called for a moratorium, precautionary pause or ban on deep-sea mining.

These findings are "another thing that we now need to take into account when it comes to deciding, 'Do we go and mine the deep ocean, or don't we?'" Sweetman says. "To me, that decision needs to be based on sound scientific advice and input."

About the Author

Allison Parshall is associate editor for mind and brain at Scientific American *and she writes the weekly online Science Quizzes. As a multimedia journalist, she contributes to* Scientific American's *podcast* Science Quickly. *Parshall's work has also appeared in Quanta Magazine and Inverse. She graduated from New York University's Arthur L. Carter Journalism Institute with a master's degree in science, health and environmental reporting. She has a bachelor's degree in psychology from Georgetown University.*

Strange Ecosystem Found Thriving below Seafloor Hydrothermal Vents

By Jack Tamisiea

There may be no ecosystem on Earth that seems less hospitable than hydrothermal vents. In the perpetual darkness, cold and relentless pressures of the deep sea, these volcanic seeps spew piping hot water so loaded with particles and metals that it looks like black smoke billowing from a chimney. But even these hellish habitats are crawling with life, ranging from giant clams and ravenous crabs to spindly octopuses and ghostly eelpout fish.

And those are just the creatures lurking above the vents. Using a deep-sea remotely operated vehicle (ROV), researchers recently flipped over slabs of seafloor to uncover a hidden ecosystem teeming with tiny life beneath the vents themselves. According to Monika Bright, a zoologist at the University of Vienna, who led the expedition, the assortment of worms, snails and microscopic larvae and bacteria that reside down here adds a new layer of complexity to hydrothermal vent ecosystems, which scientists have studied since 1977.

"We've known about the vents above for a long time, but this is basically a completely new ecosystem below," Bright says. "It's especially strange that we found it in a place that is very well studied."

Last month Bright and an international team of collaborators boarded the nonprofit Schmidt Ocean Institute's research vessel *Falkor (too)* in Panama. The scientists plumbed the depths off Central America's Pacific coast to study species ranging from symbiotic bacteria in deep-sea clams to the temperature limits of tiny copepod crustaceans.

The team focused its ROV dives on an area where diverging tectonic plates create a string of deep-sea volcanoes known as the East Pacific Rise. As the plates drift apart, magma bubbles up from the rift and cools to create new oceanic floor.

These volatile conditions fuel hydrothermal vents. Frigid water percolates through fissures in the splintering oceanic crust and meets the scalding magma below. When the seawater is heated to temperatures of more than 400 degrees Celsius, chemical reactions create a supercharged fluid that is rich in chemicals such as sulfur, and it spews out of openings in the ocean floor.

These geyserlike vents are hotspots of deep-sea diversity that can thrive in the dark, thanks to bacteria that convert chemicals into energy-providing sugars. Some of these bacteria reside inside the elongated bodies of giant tube worms (*Riftia pachyptila*). These worms, whose exposed bright-red, feathery gills make them look like six-foot-long lipstick tubes, grow in dense patches around the vents and provide habitats for other vent dwellers.

When eruptions or earthquakes alter the area's volcanic activity, these strongholds of hardy worms are wiped out. But when new hydrothermal vents pop up dozens or even hundreds of kilometers away, they are quickly colonized by towering thickets of giant tube worms within a few years.

Just how these worms arrive and anchor themselves at new vents remains unknown, Bright says. Scientists have found few tube worm larvae in the water column surrounding vents, and constant stream of supercharged fluid would also make it difficult for the larvae to attach themselves from above. This led the researchers to hypothesize that tube worm larvae were squirming through crevices below the seafloor to reach new vents.

To test this idea, the scientists sent the ROV down to the Tica Vent, a well-studied hydrothermal vent located 2,500 meters below the ocean's surface. Initially, the team glued mesh boxes over cracks in the seafloor to collect animals that moved between the rocky floor itself and the subsurface below. But when the boxes proved cumbersome, the team employed a more direct method: flipping over heavy chunks of seafloor with the ROV's robotic arm to collect what lay beneath.

This uncovered an underworld labyrinth. In a network of caves and crevices carved through the rock, the water was a balmy

25 degrees C. This provided the perfect conditions for a thriving microbial community of protists, bacteria, viruses and even some larger creatures such as snails and worms.

While the team is the first to peer below the seafloor around these hydrothermal events, its discovery is not entirely surprising to Julie Huber, a geochemist at the Woods Hole Oceanographic Institution, who was not involved in the expedition. She notes that the oceanic crust along mid-ocean ridges is porous, offering plenty of real estate for fluids, nutrients and microbes. "Given most of the animals at hydrothermal vents require all three of these things to thrive, I suppose it makes sense that animals are carving out another niche to attach themselves to and make a living," Huber says. She also thinks residing below the seafloor may help keep these tiny critters safe from prowling deep-sea crabs.

Below the vents, the researchers also discovered a lot of tiny tubes, which revealed that these subsurface chambers serve as tube worm nurseries. The scientists posit that tube worm larvae traverse this subsurface maze, which Huber refers to as the "subseafloor conveyor belt," to travel from vent to vent. The tube worms initially live down there before moving up toward the vents as they grow as much as 85 centimeters per year.

Many mysteries remain about the realm below hydrothermal vents, however. Bright and her colleagues plan to sequence the genetics of animals and microbes collected both above and below the seafloor to examine how these two ecosystems are connected. "As a scientist, you find out something, and then there [are] 10 more questions you have," Bright says.

Bright and her colleagues hope that shedding more light on the inner workings of hydrothermal vent ecosystems will help shield them from development. These areas are of potential interest to deep-sea mining companies because of the minerals that leach out of the magma-heated water as it gushes out of the vents.

That economic incentive could endanger one of the planet's most unique environments, a realm that Bright says scientists still struggle to comprehend. "From our view these vents are very extreme and exotic," she says. "But for the animals, it's not extreme to live at these pressures with fluctuating temperatures and fluctuating chemistry–it's normal."

About the Author

Jack Tamisiea is a science journalist based in Washington, D.C., who covers natural history and the environment. Follow Tamisiea on Twitter @jack_tamisiea

Ocean Discoveries Are Revising Long-Held Truths about Life

By Timothy Shank

For more than 50 years deep-sea exploration has been a continuous fount of discoveries that change how we think about life in the ocean, on dry land and even beyond our planet. Consider the following three events.

On October 16, 1968, a cable tethering the submersible Alvin to a research ship located 100 miles off Nantucket broke. The sub sank to the seafloor more than 5,000 feet below; the crew of three escaped safely. Nearly a year later, when a team brought *Alvin* back to the surface, the biggest surprise was that the crew's lunch–bologna sandwiches and apples in a plastic box–was strikingly well preserved. Bacteriological and biochemical assays proved it. Someone even took a bite. Subsequent experiments in the Woods Hole Oceanographic Institution laboratory where I'm writing this article found that rates of microbial degradation in the retrieved samples were 10 to 100 times slower than expected. This discovery, and others, led to the conclusion that metabolic and growth rates among deep-sea organisms were much slower than those of comparable species at the ocean's surface.

In 1977 scientists diving in the restored Alvin made another historic discovery–the first in-person observations of life around hot, hydrothermal vents rising from the seafloor. This sighting overturned the long-held view that our entire planetary food web was built on photosynthesis–using sunlight's energy to convert carbon dioxide and water into complex carbohydrates and oxygen. The hydrothermal organisms, and the entire ecosystem, thrived in pure darkness, converting chemicals in the vent fluid into life-sustaining compounds through a process we now call chemosynthesis.

If that revelation wasn't surprising enough, an expedition I was part of in 1993 exposed an earlier mistaken belief. We had discovered a significant hydrothermal vent ecosystem on the East Pacific Rise. The system had been destroyed by a seafloor eruption just a few years earlier, yet it had already been bountifully recolonized. A bologna sandwich might decay so slowly in the deep that you could eat it a year later, but it turned out that biological processes in the deep sea could be extremely fast as well.

Each new ocean discovery that disrupts old dogma reinforces a much larger truth: the ocean is far more complex–and much more intertwined with our own lives–than we ever imagined. For much of the 20th century, for example, scientists maintained that the deep ocean was a harsh, monotonous place of perpetual darkness, frigid temperatures, limited food and extreme pressure–conditions that should make complex forms of life impossible. But new tools for observing, sensing and sampling the deep ocean, such as increasingly sophisticated underwater vehicles with high-definition camera systems, have demonstrated that biodiversity in the darkest depths may rival that of rain forests and tropical coral reefs. These missions have further revealed that the depths are far from uniform; like kangaroo habitat in Australia and tiger lands in Asia, they are home to evolutionarily distinct biogeographic regions.

We are beginning to appreciate how connected these realms are to our own. The rapid three-dimensional change of conditions such as temperature, salinity and oxygen concentration in the deep ocean and the currents and eddies that establish the boundaries of these provinces are expected to fundamentally change as the effects of human activity reach ever farther below the surface. Already lobsters are moving to deeper, colder waters and molting at different times of the year. Commercially important groundfish such as cod and haddock are migrating poleward in search of more suitable habitat.

We are seeing that the ocean's biogeographic boundaries are neither immutable nor beyond the imprint of humans. In studies, more than half of sampled hadal organisms–those living in the deepest parts of the ocean, beyond 20,000 feet–had plastics in their gut. PCBs, which were banned in the U.S. in 1979 and phased out internationally as part of the Stockholm Convention beginning in 2001, are also common in tissues of animals from the extreme bottoms of the sea.

We are also starting to learn that life in the deep might have things to teach us. Deep-sea fish produce biomolecules called osmolytes that permit cellular functions, such as the precise folding and unfolding of proteins, to proceed unimpeded by crushing water-column pressures exceeding 15,000 pounds per square inch. Medical researchers have determined that some of these molecules could help treat Alzheimer's disease, which is characterized by misfolded proteins. In addition, decoding the genes that govern traits we see in deep-sea animals, such as those that stave off errors in DNA replication, transcription and translation, might be used in therapies for cancer and other afflictions.

The greatest paradigm that ocean exploration may tear down is that Earth represents the sole example of life in the universe. Life might have existed on Mars when it hosted liquid water, and the fact that Earth and Mars have shared ejected material in the past means we could have exchanged the building blocks of life. But the discovery of chemosynthetic life on Earth and the more recent finding of perhaps 13 liquid-water oceans underneath the icy shells of moons such as Jupiter's Europa and Saturn's Enceladus–places that may have been too distant to have shared life-bearing material with Earth in the past–raise the possibility of a second, independent genesis of life. And if life can form twice in one solar system, then it could be anywhere we look in the heavens.

About the Author

Timothy Shank is a biologist, director of the Molecular Ecology and Evolution Lab at Woods Hole Oceanographic Institution, and co-leader of the Deep-Ocean Genomes Project.

Bizarro Life-Forms Inhabiting Deep-Sea Vents May Be at Risk

By Shannon Hall

Two years ago, Shana Goffredi raced to the control room of the R/V *Western Flyer*, a 117-foot-long research ship in the Gulf of California. Television monitors onboard the vessel displayed what looked like an alien world near the ocean bottom, and Goffredi wanted to get a better look. On screen were thousands of tiny orange tube worms and dozens of other animals, some of which were new to science. The bizarre habitat gleamed in the lights of an underwater robotic probe as it explored the environs of a seafloor spring spewing water at superhot temperatures–known as a hydrothermal vent. What struck Goffredi, a marine biologist at Occidental College, along with the 10 other scientists onboard was how different the life-forms at this site, called the Pescadero Basin, looked from those at a neighboring site. Some 75 kilometers away in the same gulf, vents within the Alarcón Rise also hosted masses of tube worms, only they were blood-red in color. Overall, the two sites shared only seven out of 61 animal species identified. "There's nowhere else in the world where you have this dramatic difference of species at this close of a place," says Shannon Johnson, an MBARI researcher who was also onboard that day.

Recent research has hinted that neighboring hydrothermal vents might host different arrays of life, but the scene in the Gulf of California, as Goffredi, Johnson and their colleagues described it in the July 26 *Proceedings of the Royal Society B* (pdf),provides one of the first dramatic examples of this trend. Goffredi's team thinks the local geology and chemistry of each vent effectively selects for a rare and specialized animal community that may only be able to live at that site.

The search for these hot waters began in 2012 when MBARI scientists sent a missile-shaped underwater drone to map the

Pescadero Basin following a discovery of chemical anomalies that suggested the presence of vents. Although the drone was able to find them, it lacked instruments that could image any animal communities. So, in April 2015 MBARI scientists sent down an SUV-size remotely operated vehicle to take footage of the vents and collect samples of the surrounding seawater, mud, rocks and animals. It was during this cruise that Goffredi and Johnson found themselves glued to the incoming images. And they were not alone. "All of us were out of our seats, taking pictures of the screens with our phones," Johnson says. "We looked like a bunch of tourists!"

Although it was immediately evident to everyone onboard that the animals found at vents within the Pescadero Basin were radically different from those found at the neighboring Alarcón Rise, scientists could not immediately explain why. *Riftia*, the blood-red tubeworms seen at the Alarcón Rise, are known to travel great distances. Not only have they been spotted in the Gulf of California, they have also been found in the Galápagos Archipelago and near Easter Island. Although that in itself was initially a mystery, scientists now know these animals release tiny larvae that get carried by ocean currents to different vents, where they settle and form a new colony. Still, their exact movements remain unknown. In recent years it was thought that *Riftia* and other vent organisms might migrate in a stepwise manner, moving from one vent to the immediate neighboring vent and so on. But the new work by Goffredi's team suggests the larvae will not settle for any old vent. "They're kind of like Goldilocks," Johnson says. "They have to find the right environment to be comfortable and thrive."

In fact, the itinerant next generation might die if it encounters any vent with radically different geology and chemistry from its home vent. Larvae can travel great distances, but they might have to skip neighboring vents should they be, say, too hot or too cold, and venture farther to seek a suitable home. In seas that are well populated with vents that will not be a problem, but in a sparsely populated area it gets trickier—and every vent becomes more critical, says Cindy Van Dover, a deep-sea biologist and director of the Duke University Marine Laboratory, who was not involved in the discovery.

Not every expert agrees with the biogeochemistry hypothesis. Richard Thomson, a physical oceanographer at the Institute of Ocean Sciences in British Columbia who also did not take part in the work, says that deep-sea currents could be the driving factor behind the extreme variations in biology. Perhaps currents rushing down into the Pescadero Basin are so strong that the habitat is only suitable to the hardiest tubeworms. Or maybe the true culprit is time. Tim Shank, a deep-sea biologist at Woods Hole Oceanographic Institution in Massachusetts, suggests a site might not contain animals for the simple reason that they have not arrived yet. Shank compares the vents with a forest. If you cut it down, grasses and other shrubs will grow long before new trees do. That does not mean those trees cannot grow in that forest. Still, Shank thinks, because the diversity between the two sites is so vast, it is likely geochemistry plays the largest role. He was not part of the study but is excited to see further research in the area that can better develop that hypothesis.

Regardless of the cause of the distinct populations at the vents, the new research suggests these animal populations might be more fragile than suspected, which raises a looming concern. Several companies are applying for permits to mine the Gulf of California seafloor for precious metals, including gold and platinum. Mining machinery could destroy some of these worlds in the process of generating high returns on ores. But for Van Dover, that value cannot compare with the richness of the thriving animal communities inhabiting Earth's hydrothermal vents. "When I look at the pictures of these beautiful, rich populations and just imagine someone happily going in and scraping it clean, that seems to me pretty tragic," she says. And mining companies could pose a risk not only to a single vent colony, but to ones farther up and down the ridge. Because these animals rely on vents as stepping-stones to establish new colonies, eliminating one vent might stop a species in its tracks. "If you blew the critical habitat, then that's going to be a problem for that species," Van Dover says. No scientist yet knows which habitats are critical for vent organisms or how many vents can be destroyed before the connectivity with other vents along the ridge is lost. But if we break this chain, Van Dover says, we cannot fix it.

About the Author

Shannon Hall is an award-winning freelance science journalist based in the Rocky Mountains. She specializes in writing about astronomy, geology and the environment.

Mysterious Galápagos Reefs Harbor Strawberry Squid and Other Fantastic Creatures

By Jack Tamisiea

The Galápagos Islands are famed as a bizarre menagerie of blue-footed boobies, giant tortoises and seafaring iguanas. But the waters surrounding the archipelago are also brimming with biodiversity, including nearly 3,000 species ranging from pint-size penguins to colossal whale sharks.

And now researchers have discovered yet another trove of life's diversity in the Galápagos, this one in a dark, frigid world more than 400 meters below the waves. The team used a remotely operated vehicle (ROV) to map two pristine cold-water coral reefs—one of which is the size of eight football fields—and two submerged volcanoes, or seamounts, in high resolution. These abyssal reefs, which may be thousands of years old, are teeming with sharks, squid and a variety of other creatures.

The new discovery provides a detailed glimpse of the region's overlooked assortment of cold-water corals, says Katleen Robert, a researcher specializing in seafloor mapping at the Fisheries and Marine Institute of Memorial University of Newfoundland. Robert led an international team of collaborators aboard the nonprofit Schmidt Ocean Institute's research vessel *Falkor (too)* during the 30-day mapping expedition, which began in September. (Previous expeditions on the vessel have recorded baby octopuses hatching in a surprise deep-sea nursery and a strange ecosystem under the seafloor.)

The reefs and seamounts lie within the Galápagos Marine Reserve (GMR), a swath of the eastern Pacific Ocean spanning some 133,000 square kilometers. The area, about 1,000 kilometers west of Ecuador, sits at the intersection of three major ocean currents;

the resulting influx of drifting life forms and nutrients has helped it develop one of the planet's most biodiverse marine habitats.

Very little was known about the ecosystems in the GMR's deeper reaches, so one of the team's main goals was to chart their layout. According to Robert, most deep-sea mapping uses acoustic methods because sound spreads more easily through water than light does from far distances. But at closer ranges, measuring with laser beams instead of sound waves creates a much higher-resolution map of the seafloor's rugged topography. So the team deployed the ROV *SuBastian* to get close enough to bounce lasers off of the two reefs, located between 370 and 420 meters below the surface.

As *SuBastian* explored the reefs, the researchers used the cutting-edge laser scanning technology to craft maps of this hidden environment with a resolution of down to two millimeters. The maps were so detailed that the scientists aboard the research vessel could pinpoint individual animals and make out minute details of the corals' anatomy.

When the researchers return to the site in the future, Robert says, they could even use this mapping technique to measure the corals' elusive growth rates. "Cold-water corals grow very slowly, like a few millimeters a year over hundreds of years," she says. "If you want to see the corals grow, you really have to be able to have that really high resolution that our laser scanner is able to provide."

The vast sizes of these reefs—one covers a whopping 800-meter-long stretch of the seafloor, while the other spans more than 250 meters—led the researchers to posit that corals have been living here for hundreds, and possibly thousands, of years.

Unlike the better-known shallow coral reefs that thrive in balmy, sunlit waters, cold-water corals thrive hundreds to thousands of meters beneath the surface—often in frigid waters with little to no light. Instead of relying on photosynthetic algae for energy, the polyps of these corals catch tiny organisms floating in the water. This allows them to build lush coral gardens that act like an oasis in the dark.

As the team mapped the reefs, it identified more than 40 different varieties of cold-water corals, some of which were covered with eggs. The corals were also crawling with critters, including squat lobsters, feathery brittle stars, and dense patches of anemones and sponges. Several species of fish patrolled the reefs, including skates, sharks and ratfish, whose large, emerald-green eyes gather the scant light available in these inky depths. The scientists also found a variety of animals swimming above the reefs, including strawberry squid, whose mismatched eyes help them simultaneously search for prey above and below them.

As *SuBastian* collected samples of these deep-sea denizens, scientists aboard the *Falkor (too)* measured the area's currents and water conditions. The two new reefs both occupy a layer of the water column with a low concentration of oxygen. Robert says future work is needed to determine why deep-sea corals cluster in such areas.

She believes the discovery of the new reefs is a major step in understanding and protecting these little-known seafloor environments throughout the eastern Pacific. Though the GMR reefs are protected, other similar ecosystems may be threatened by activities such as deep-sea mining. As Robert puts it, "We need to know that these reefs are there before we can realize what we can lose."

About the Author

Jack Tamisiea is a science journalist based in Washington, D.C., who covers natural history and the environment. Follow Tamisiea on Twitter @jack_tamisiea

Seals Show Scientists an Unknown Antarctic Canyon

By Ethan Freedman

Humans have sailed the oceans' surfaces for millennia, but their depths remain effectively uncharted. Only about a quarter of the seafloor has been mapped at high resolution. Maps of most regions display only approximate depths and often miss entire underwater mountains or canyons.

So a group of researchers has recruited some deep-diving experts: Elephant Seals and Weddell Seals. Scientists have been placing trackers on these blubbery marine mammals around Antarctica for years, gathering data on ocean temperature and salinity. For a new study, the researchers compared these dives' location and depth data with some of the less detailed seafloor maps. They spotted places where the seals dove deeper than should have been possible according to the maps—meaning the existing depth estimates were inaccurate.

In eastern Antarctica's Vincennes Bay, the diving seals helped the scientists find a large, hidden underwater canyon plunging to depths of more than a mile. An Australian research ship called the RSV *Nuyina* later measured the canyon's exact depth using sonar, and the researchers have proposed naming their find the Mirounga-Nuyina Canyon—honoring both the ship and the involved Elephant Seals, genus *Mirounga*.

"The seals discovered the canyon, and the ship confirmed it," says Clive McMahon, a researcher at the Integrated Marine Observing System in Australia and a co-author of the new study, published in *Communications Earth & Environment*.

But seals can't map the entire ocean floor. The trackers used in the study could pinpoint a seal's geographical location only within about 1.5 miles, which allows for useful but not exactly high-resolution data. Plus, because the seals don't always dive to the bottom of the ocean, they can reveal only where the bottom is deeper than in existing maps—not shallower. McMahon notes that scientists could improve on these data by using more precise GPS trackers and analyzing the seals' diving patterns to determine whether they have reached the seafloor or simply stopped descending.

The current seal-dive data can still be valuable for an important task, says Anna Wåhlin, an oceanographer at the University of Gothenburg in Sweden, who was not involved in the new research. The deep ocean around Antarctica is warmer than the frigid waters at the surface, and seafloor canyons can allow that warmer water to flow to the ice along the continent's coast, Wåhlin explains. To predict how Antarctica's ice will melt, scientists will need to know where those canyons are and how deep they go.

About the Author

Ethan Freedman is a science and nature journalist based in New York City who reports on climate, ecology, the future and the built environment.

The Ocean's Wilderness Areas Are Smaller Than You Think—and They're Disappearing Fast

By Kendall Jones & James Watson

The ocean covers more than 70 percent of our planet, an area of over 160 million square miles. It is so immense that explorers once thought there was no way to cross it. When our ships were advanced enough to do so, naturalists then thought it impossible for humans to ever exhaust fisheries or drive marine species to extinction.

They were wrong.

Commercial fishing now covers an area four times that of agriculture, and much of that expanse has been rendered completely unsustainable. We have depleted 90 percent of formerly important coastal species. Large fish have been harvested so heavily that they are virtually wiped out in many places. Indeed, studying once vital fish habitats such as coral reefs has been compared to trying to understand the Serengeti by studying termites and locusts while ignoring the wildebeest and lions.

Some may hope that there are immense areas still untouched, given that humans do not live on the ocean and we need specialized ships to go far beyond the coast. But that is incorrect. In a study published this summer in *Current Biology*, we used fine-scale global data on 15 human stressors to the ocean–including commercial shipping, sediment runoff and several types of fishing–to show that Earth's "marine wilderness" is dwindling. Just 13 percent of the ocean remains as wilderness, and in coastal regions, where human activities are most intense, there is almost no wilderness left at all. Of the roughly 21 million square miles of marine wilderness remaining, almost all is found in the Arctic and Antarctic or around remote Pacific island nations with low populations.

These remnants of wilderness are home to unparalleled marine life, sustaining large predators and high levels of genetic diversity. The lack of human impact can also make them highly resilient to rising sea temperatures and coral bleaching–stressors that cannot be halted without globally coordinated efforts to reduce emissions.

In an era of widespread marine biodiversity loss, wilderness areas also act like a window into the past, revealing what the ocean looked like before overfishing and pollution took their toll. This is crucial information for marine conservation. If we are to restore degraded areas to their former state, we need to know what to aim for.

What concerns us now is that most wilderness remains unprotected. This means it could be lost at any time, as advances in technology allow us to fish deeper and ship farther than ever before. Thanks to a warming climate, even places that were once safeguarded because of year-round ice cover are now open to fishing and shipping.

This lack of protection stems in large part from international environmental policies failing to recognize the unique values of wilderness, instead focusing on saving at-risk ecosystems and avoiding extinctions. This is akin to a government using its entire health budget on emergency cardiac surgery, without preemptive policies encouraging exercise to decrease the risk of heart attacks occurring in the first place.

If Earth's marine biodiversity is to be preserved in perpetuity, it is time for conservation to focus not only on the E.R. but also on preventive health measures.

Our *Current Biology* paper comes with a plea. As we develop international conservation agreements, it is crucial that we recognize the unique values of wilderness and set targets for its retention. Without further action, wilderness areas will likely be lost forever–something President Lyndon B. Johnson urged us to avoid when he signed the Wilderness Act in 1964. "If future generations are to remember us with gratitude rather than contempt," Johnson observed, "we must leave them more than the miracles of technology. We must leave them a glimpse of the world as it was in the beginning."

About the Authors

Kendall Jones is a conservation planning specialist with Wildlife Conservation Society

James Watson is a professor of conservation science at the University of Queensland and Director of the Science and Research Initiative at Wildlife Conservation Society

Four New Octopus Species Discovered in the Deep Sea

By Ashley Balzer Vigil

Last month a team of scientists visited an ethereal nursery on the seafloor off Costa Rica, where they watched in awe as a new generation of deep-sea octopuses gently emerged from a quivering cluster of oblong, semitranslucent eggs.

Now the researchers have confirmed these deep-sea dwellers are members of an entirely new, yet-to-be-named species, nicknamed the "Dorado octopus." And they have announced they've discovered three more new deep-sea octopus species on top of that.

"Finding four new species of octopuses on just two expeditions is exciting, revealing some of the rich biodiversity of the deep sea and hinting at how much more waits to be discovered," says Jim Barry, a deep-sea ecologist at the Monterey Bay Aquarium Research Institute, who was not involved in the expeditions.

The nursery visit last December was part two of a Schmidt Ocean Institute expedition that took place six months earlier. Then, too, researchers witnessed baby deep-sea octopuses emerge from eggs that their respective mothers were brooding near hydrothermal vents on the same underwater rock formation, called the Dorado Outcrop (hence the new species' nickname). The octopuses' proximity to the vents suggests these creatures may have evolved to use warmth from the seeping hydrothermal fluid to accelerate the incubation process–which is notoriously long for many deep-sea creatures, leaving their offspring vulnerable to predators for extended periods.

The team collected some octopus specimens near the vents and others farther away and brought them to the Zoology Museum at the University of Costa Rica. Fiorella Vásquez, a research assistant at the Zoology Museum, and Janet Voight, associate curator of invertebrate zoology at the Field Museum of Natural History in Chicago, then set out to classify the creatures.

The Dorado octopus is remarkably similar to the pearl octopus (*Muusoctopus robustus*), which a separate team of researchers previously found brooding eggs near hydrothermal vents off central California. To distinguish the Dorado octopus as a separate species in the recent investigation, the scientists made careful observations and descriptions of the different octopuses, such as measuring their arms and enumerating their suckers. "The two species share an unusual morphology, having smallish eyes, a robust body and fairly short arms," Voight explains. "It's the details that separate them."

Of the three additional species the team identified farther from the hydrothermal vents, two are also members of the genus Muusoctopus. They have double rows of suckers on their arms and lack an ink sac––other traits that are characteristic of the genus.

"But they look really different," Voight says of these two species. For both, large eyes are the most obvious difference from the Dorado octopus. And one of the species is reddish, with long arms, while the other has a lighter shade on its top side and a darker one underneath.

The fourth species is an oddball. "It was just so unlike anything I had seen; I didn't know where to assign it," Voight says. But she and Vásquez observed a single row of suckers on each of the animal's arms and strange bumps on its skin, which they say could place this species in the genus Graneledone. Voight notes, however, that "its bumps aren't quite like what I expected to see, and it's really pale-colored, so it's a bit of an enigma."

These three other newfound species are also officially nameless so far. The researchers collected additional specimens that they're still poring over to determine the best classifications. Subsequently they'll have to meticulously describe and illustrate each species, run that information through peer review and then, if accepted, the species names will enter the scientific literature.

"We have so much to explore in the deep ocean, and part of that exploration is to find new species," Vásquez says. "Every step we take to learn a little more about what is at the bottom of our ocean will help us to conserve it."

The expedition also identified a rare deep-sea skate nursery—which the scientists are calling Skate Park—and three new hydrothermal springs. Expedition co-leader Jorge Cortés-Núñez, a professor emeritus of biology at the University of Costa Rica, says "we have samples and data for many years to come, motivation to continue along that line of research, and powerful information and images to justify the protection and conservation of the deep sea, not only of Costa Rica but of all the ocean."

About the Author

Ashley Balzer Vigil writes about astrophysics for NASA's Goddard Space Flight Center by day and moonlights as a freelance environmental writer.

The Mystery of Milky Seas Is Finally Being Solved

By Michelle Nijhuis

On January 30, 1864, the Confederate warship CSS *Alabama* entered what its captain described as a "remarkable patch of the sea." The *Alabama*, sailing southwest along the Horn of Africa, was one of several Confederate vessels cruising the world's oceans during the U.S. Civil War, weakening the Union by raiding its merchant ships. Formidable pirates though they were, Captain Raphael Semmes and his crew were spooked by the sea they encountered that January evening. "At about eight P.M., there being no moon, but the sky being clear, and the stars shining brightly, we suddenly passed from the deep blue water in which we had been sailing, into a patch of water so white that it startled me," Semmes recounted in a memoir.

At first he thought that the pale, constant glow indicated a submerged ridge, but a weighted line the crew dropped over the gunwale sank for 600 feet without hitting bottom. "Around the horizon there was a subdued glare, or flush, as though there were a distant illumination going on, whilst overhead there was a lurid, dark sky," Semmes wrote. "The whole face of nature seemed changed, and with but little stretch of the imagination, the *Alabama* might have been conceived to be a phantom ship, lighted up by the sickly and unearthly glare of a phantom sea." The *Alabama* traveled through the eerie water for several hours, finally exiting the patch as abruptly as it had entered it.

Semmes's firsthand description is one of the earliest reliable accounts of such a sea, and it has become a valuable, though inadvertent, contribution to science. Now, after combining dozens of historical reports with state-of-the-art satellite data, researchers are close to solving one of the ocean's most persistent mysteries–its vast, ephemeral displays of ghostly living light.

Silent Dread

The cold radiance emitted by fireflies, some species of fungi and various sea creatures is called bioluminescence. Although it is one of the oldest subjects of scientific study, it is also among the most elusive. Mentions of animal light appear in ancient poetry and songs from many cultures. In the third century B.C.E., Aristotle noticed that if he struck the surface of the sea with a rod, the water sometimes produced a bright blue flash. Three hundred years later Pliny the Elder described light-emitting species of mollusks, jellyfish and mushrooms, adding that the Black Forest of central Europe was rumored to glow with bioluminescent birds (such rumors, though often repeated, were unfortunately never confirmed).

Around 1370 Egyptian zoologist Al-Damiri included bioluminescent insects in his zoological dictionary. And in 1492, during his fateful approach to the Bahamas, Christopher Columbus observed glimmers of light in the ocean–an occurrence that scientists now surmise was produced by bioluminescent marine worms of the genus *Odontosyllis*, which periodically rise to the water's surface en masse to perform a circular mating "dance." In the late 1800s, after centuries of speculation, scientists confirmed that bioluminescence results from an oxidation reaction between an enzyme and its substrate within animal and plant cells. Basic questions remained, however: no one knew what prompted different organisms to glow or what purpose the light might serve.

Most accounts of bioluminescence, on land and at sea, describe blue-green flashes and gleams, sometimes stimulated by disturbance, as with Aristotle's rod. But reports such as that of Captain Semmes suggested a very different phenomenon. The seawater plied by sailors was suffused with steady white light, not bluish bursts, and the glow often stretched for miles. These "milky seas" were rare enough, and strange enough, that people widely considered them to be tall tales–more plausible than mermaid encounters, perhaps, but just barely so. Herman Melville, in his 1851 epic *Moby-Dick*, portrayed them as bad omens, describing a mariner's "silent, superstitious dread" on entering a "midnight sea of milky whiteness," as if "shoals of combed white bears were swimming round him." In Jules Verne's novel *Twenty Thousand Leagues Under the Sea*, written almost two decades later, the fictional marine biologist Pierre Aronnax is less perturbed by his voyage through a milky sea in the Bay of Bengal, calmly informing his assistant that "the whiteness which surprises you is caused only by the presence of myriads of infusoria, a sort of luminous little worm, gelatinous and without color."

Verne's pilot was on the right track, but it would be more than a century before science began to catch up with science fiction. In July 1985 a U.S. Navy research vessel encountered a milky sea off the Arabian Peninsula. The scientists onboard, who were conducting a broad study of marine bioluminescence, were equipped for this stroke of luck, and they quickly collected seawater samples for inspection. In addition to the dinoflagellates, copepods and other types of plankton associated with the familiar, flashing displays, the samples contained bioluminescent bacteria. The researchers suggested that milky seas occurred after algae colonies on the water's surface bloomed and died. When the dead algal cells ruptured, they released lipids subsequently consumed by bacteria, which then multiplied furiously, eventually becoming concentrated enough to produce a continuous glow.

Finally, milky seas had been established as a scientific phenomenon with a biological cause. But to understand where, when and exactly why they occurred, researchers needed more data than serendipity could provide.

Sailing over Snow

For the U.S. Navy, marine bioluminescence is a practical concern because a patch of bright seawater can outline a submarine, turning it into an easy target. In the early 2000s Steven Miller, an atmospheric scientist then at the Naval Research Laboratory in Monterey, Calif., began to wonder whether satellite sensors could detect bioluminescence from above. The only sensors capable of observing visible light at night were those in the Operational Line Scan (OLS) system that flew on U.S. Air Force satellites. Miller knew that most surface displays of marine bioluminescence were much too small to register on the sensors, so, on a whim, he searched the Internet for mentions of widespread bioluminescence. He turned up a description of milky seas on the Web site Science Frontiers, an idiosyncratic catalog of "unusual & unexplained" happenings then maintained by physicist William R. Corliss.

Miller, his curiosity piqued, began to collect eyewitness accounts. Among them was a relatively recent report from a British merchant ship, the *SS Lima*, which had sailed through a milky sea along the Horn of Africa on January 25, 1995. "The bioluminescence appeared to cover the entire sea area, from horizon to horizon," read the *Lima*'s log entry, "and it appeared as though the ship was sailing over a field of snow or gliding over the clouds."

When Miller pulled up the OLS images from the *Lima*'s location on that date, he initially saw nothing. But when he zoomed in, he saw a faint, comma-shaped smear. "It looked like a finger smudge, but it moved as I moved the figure," he remembers. Miller found that the edges of the smudge matched the coordinates noted in the ship's log as it entered and exited the milky sea, which covered nearly 5,500 square miles. When he examined OLS images from the days immediately before and after the *Lima*'s encounter, he found the same smudge, rotating counterclockwise in concert with local ocean currents. "Okay," Miller thought, "we *can* see bioluminescence from space."

Miller got in touch with Steven Haddock, a marine biologist at the nearby Monterey Bay Aquarium Research Institute (MBARI), to share his findings. Like Miller, Haddock had never seen a milky sea firsthand, but he was familiar with the phenomenon, especially because one of his mentors, marine biologist Peter Herring (now retired), had cataloged hundreds of descriptions of milky seas dating back to Captain Semmes and the *Alabama*. Haddock, who primarily studies bioluminescence in jellyfish, had spent much of his career trying to get as close as possible to bioluminescent organisms using crewed or remotely operated deep-sea submersibles. He and Miller began to collaborate.

Although the OLS detection from 1995 had been something of a fluke—the product of Miller's persistence and a fortuitous satellite position—Miller hoped a new, more sensitive low-light visible-spectrum instrument called the day-night band (DNB) sensor would allow a systematic survey of milky seas. The sensor, launched in 2011, now rides on two satellites more than 500 miles above Earth's surface, each orbiting the planet daily. More than 100 times as sensitive as the OLS, the DNB can easily pick up the gleam of a milky sea. But it can also pick up the faint "airglow" produced by the absorption of ultraviolet light in the upper atmosphere, some of which is reflected by clouds. "There were clouds everywhere. The airglow is emitting upward, and sometimes it makes this really diffuse, widespread veil of light," Miller explains. Differentiating bioluminescence from these other phenomena, he adds, "took us many years of looking at what seemed like very noisy imagery."

Thanks to the long history of sightings by mariners, Miller and Haddock knew that the occurrences of milky seas peaked in winter and summer and that they were most often reported in the northwestern Indian Ocean, where both the *Alabama* and the *Lima* had encountered them, as well as around Indonesia, in particular near the island of Java and in the Banda Sea. Narrowing his search to these seasons and locations, Miller analyzed DNB data collected on moonless nights from 2012 through 2021, eventually identifying a dozen events that were not clouds or airglow, were invisible during the day and drifted with the currents over multiple nights. One 2019 event, detected just south of Java, was visible for at least 45 nights and covered almost 40,000 square miles—an area the size of Kentucky. Its multiweek persistence suggests that the DNB sensor could be used to dispatch researchers to newly formed milky seas in time to conduct dives in them. "[There's] only so much you can do from spaceborne measurement," Miller says. "You can't get into the water, you can't see the vertical structure of the glow within water, you can't sample the critters, you can't measure the detailed chemistry. [For] all these things, you need to be in the middle of it to truly understand."

While Miller waits for the chance to be in the middle of a milky sea, he continues to expand his collection of sightings. A recent addition comes from Sam Keck Scott, who in the summer of 2010 helped to sail a restored Dutch ketch from Malta to Singapore, crossing the Arabian Sea. One evening in late July, as Scott began his watch, he noticed an odd radiance in the air. After a few minutes he realized that even though the sky was completely dark he could see the boat's sails and hull; the entire ocean had brightened and seemed to be shining from within. Scott and his crewmates sailed through the milky sea for about four hours, exiting it even more suddenly than they had entered. "We knew it was bioluminescence of some kind, but it was on this wild, wild scale, unlike anything I'd ever seen before," Scott recalls.

Burglar Alarm

From a distance, scientists have proposed various hypotheses about how milky seas form. Investigators on the 1985 navy expedition theorized that the bioluminescent bacteria they collected had congregated around an algal bloom. Other sleuths have since suggested that the steady glow results from "quorum sensing," the ability of bacteria to communicate through chemical signaling. Once their density is high enough to produce a perceptible collective glow, they sustain a continual shine. But why? Some biologists think bioluminescence in other marine organisms helps them attract food or mates or functions as a kind of burglar alarm, flashing when they are under attack in hopes of attracting the predators of their predators. The glow of quorum sensing in bacteria may act as a different invitation: when a colony runs low on food in the open water, it may glow to encourage nearby fish to come and consume the bacteria, consequently sustaining the bacteria in their guts.

The decade of DNB data complicates the idea that milky seas occur most frequently in winter and late summer. The peaks in milky-sea formation do appear to be strongest in the northwestern Indian Ocean when winter and summer monsoons trigger phytoplankton blooms by bringing deep, cold, nutrient-rich water to the sea surface. Farther east, however, milky seas may be set up by the Indian Ocean Dipole, an El Niño–like pattern of sea-surface temperatures associated with cool, dry conditions and strong winds in the eastern Indian Ocean between May and October. The satellite data also suggest an explanation for why the glow occasionally seems to extend to some depth, creating the perception among mariners that their ship is suddenly floating in light: Miller found that several milky seas occurred in the relative calm between large ocean eddies, where a combination of currents and temperature gradients can isolate a column of seawater from the surrounding ocean, putting it at a standstill. Such conditions, he hypothesizes, could foster superdense bacterial populations whose quorum sensing extends vertically as well as horizontally to adjacent colonies, magnifying the depth and breadth of the resulting milky sea.

Miller and Haddock hope the DNB sensors' ability to detect–and, in time, perhaps predict–milky seas will allow researchers to quickly head out to the ocean and collect samples to test hypotheses. Until then, milky seas are unlikely to give up their lingering mysteries.

Everywhere Aglow

The secrets of milky seas persist in part because much larger questions remain about the nature, function and extent of bioluminescence itself. Since most bioluminescent organisms live in the ocean, many at great depths, observing bioluminescence firsthand has required considerable resources–and not inconsiderable risk. Marine biologist Edith Widder, who founded the Ocean Research and Conservation Association in 2005, began her pioneering bioluminescence studies in the 1980s. She recounts her numerous and occasionally hair-raising submersible experiences–including a life-threatening leak at a depth of 350 feet–in her 2021 book, *Below the Edge of Darkness*. "I've spent a lot of my career in submersibles, operating in the dark" because only very recently have cameras been able to perceive both the light and the color of bioluminescence, she told me. "It's absolutely, breathtakingly beautiful, and finally [other people are] getting to see it."

Widder and other researchers who have managed to take deep-sea voyages have known for decades that bioluminescence is a common ability. But the first reliable estimate of its occurrence came in 2017, when Haddock and Séverine Martini, then a postdoctoral researcher at MBARI and now at the Mediterranean Institute of Oceanography, published an analysis of 17 years of video observations collected by remotely operated vehicles off the California coast. From more than 350,000 observations, which included more than 500 groups of organisms, taken at depths from just below the surface to nearly 13,000 feet, Martini and Haddock concluded that at least three quarters of the organisms were capable of bioluminescence. The percentage remained remarkably consistent at different ocean depths. In a 2019 study, they found that about a third of the organisms living on the ocean floor are bioluminescent. Martini identified a carnivorous sponge that was not only new to science but the first documented case of bioluminescence in its phylum.

Given that the ocean is the largest living space on the planet, the two analyses suggest that bioluminescence is one of the predominant ecological traits on Earth. "It's not something far away that you'll never see in your life," Martini says. "At sea, everything is glowing–you just have to pay attention." For Martini, Haddock, Widder and the few other marine bioluminescence researchers, the pervasive glow only increases their interest in its ecological functions, evolutionary history, chemistry and genetics–and their excitement about the high-definition underwater cameras and advanced genetic sequencing that offer new ways of accessing a once all but inaccessible world.

Humans have benefited greatly from bioluminescent species. Medical and biological researchers frequently use green fluorescent protein, which biologists isolated from bioluminescent jellyfish in the 1960s, as a visual marker of proteins and the components of living cells. Widder is using bioluminescent bacteria to identify pollution hotspots in Florida's Indian River Lagoon, one of the most diverse estuaries in North America. Fertilizer and pesticide runoff from farms and lawns, as well as leakage from sewage and septic systems, has been poisoning the lagoon for decades, and the pollution has accumulated in its sediments. Because most pollutants interfere with bacterial respiration and therefore with bacterial bioluminescence, Widder and her colleagues have taken sediments from the lagoon and mixed them with bioluminescent bacteria in the lab to determine the relative concentrations of pollutants throughout the lagoon–knowledge that helps in monitoring, mitigation and restoration efforts.

Although applications are expanding, the ability of marine organisms to benefit from their own bioluminescent capacity is under threat. The rush to mine valuable metals from the ocean floor is expected to tremendously impact not only the seabed but the entire deep sea, where the water is typically clear enough for bioluminescent organisms to communicate with one another across hundreds of feet. When robotic mining vehicles scrape the seafloor, they kick up clouds of sediment. After machines pump collected material to the surface and remove the fist-sized, metal-rich nodules, they dump the remaining mud and silt back into the sea, again clouding once transparent water–inevitably disrupting communication among the bioluminescent organisms and interfering with their ability to find food and mates.

"In the context of ocean ecology and ocean health, it's important to understand how widespread and widely used [bioluminescence] is," says Haddock, who co-authored a 2020 paper on the ecological effects of deep-sea mining. "If you do something that's going to affect that process, it's going to have all these ripple effects that we can only now start to appreciate." The glowing seas that so terrified generations of mariners have taken no victims and left no traces; the cloudy seas created by humans, however, could permanently dim the ocean's light.

About the Author

Michelle Nijhuis is author of Beloved Beasts: Fighting for Life in an Age of Extinction *(W. W. Norton, 2021), a history of the modern conservation movement. She lives in Washington State.*

Bizarre Ecosystem Discovered More Than Two Miles beneath Arctic Ocean

By Claire Cameron

Deep down in the Arctic Ocean, life becomes bizarre. One might suppose that at its greatest depths, the icy, dark water would be inhospitable to much—but a new discovery reminds us that that is far from the case.

Off the coast of Greenland, the deep seafloor is littered with towering mounds made of crystallized methane and other gases. Known as the Freya hydrate mounds, these structures act like a "frozen reef," a haven for creatures that have evolved to live in environments unlike any other on Earth.

In a new paper published in *Nature Communications*, scientists document the deepest ever found of these mounds, at 3,640 meters—or some 2.26 miles—below the surface. The discovery was made as part of the Ocean Census Arctic Deep–EXTREME24 expedition to explore and research the Arctic environment and document ocean life using tools such as underwater robots.

Incredibly, the mounds, which are also known as gas hydrate cold seeps, release methane gas flares some 3,300 meters up into the water—the tallest such flares ever recorded. Over time the mounds collapse and reform, a dynamic process that the researchers say gives insights into the Arctic's various ecosystems.

"These are not static deposits," Giuliana Panieri, a study co-author and a professor at the Arctic University of Norway, said in a statement about the new research. "They are living geological features, responding to tectonics, deep heat flow, and environmental change."

Gathered at the mounds are chemosynthetic creatures—life that has evolved to depend not on sun-powered photosynthesis for food but on chemical reactions instead. Some of the creatures seen at the Freya mounds are also found at hydrothermal vents, or fissures in the seafloor through which hot, chemical-laden water erupts, the researchers said, suggesting these ecosystems may be more intertwined than previously thought.

"The links that we have found between life at this seep and hydrothermal vents in the Arctic indicate that these island-like habitats on the ocean floor will need to be protected from any future impacts of deep-sea mining in the region," said Jon Copley, a study co-author and a professor at the University of Southampton in England, in the same statement.

About the Author

Claire Cameron is breaking news chief at Scientific American. Originally from Scotland, she moved to New York City in 2012. Her work has appeared in National Geographic, Slate, Inc. Magazine, Nautilus, Semafor, and elsewhere.

See the Lush Kelp Forests Scientists Are Fighting for as Oceans Warm

By Avery Schuyler Nunn

While free diving to photograph kelp forests along the California coastline, I've viscerally felt the consequences of finiteness as a living being–the fleeting nature of a single breath, the limits of my own lungs. Kelp forests, too, have a threshold. These towering underwater jungles, which unfurl in golden ribbons with the pull of the tides, exhale life-giving oxygen into the sea, sequester carbon, shelter other organisms, buffer shorelines and remain the basis of life for many marine worlds. But along the North American coasts, heat waves, sea star wasting diseases, declining sea otter numbers and surging urchin populations have stripped away vast kelp canopies, leaving barren seascapes underneath the waves: rocky crags devoid of life except for the kelp-devouring sea urchins. In some regions, more than 90 percent of these forests have disappeared within only the past 10 years. Some Indigenous communities, who have long understood kelp's role as both refuge and lifeline, describe the plant as the ocean's "veins," carrying life through the currents. Now the pulse is fading.

And yet scientists are studying kelp not just as a casualty of climate change but as a survivor. "Diving into the kelp forest is like falling into a dream," says Sara T. Gonzalez, a researcher at the Woods Hole Oceanographic Institution. "But above all the magic of the kelp forest, what really motivated me to study kelp was its dual importance as an essential habitat for fish and invertebrates and as a valued natural resource in human society."

Gonzalez's team is tapping into the remarkable resilience written in kelp's DNA. In a recent study in the *Journal of Applied Phycology*, the researchers identified sugar kelp strains with natural genetic adaptations that help them withstand rising ocean temperatures. By crossbreeding heat-tolerant gametophytes–the microscopic precursors of adult kelp, as well as other algae and plants–from different species, they produced organisms that thrived under heat stress. Because gametophytes are crucial to kelp breeding, and because this resistance seems to be passed to offspring, the development could contribute to both wild kelp restoration and seaweed farming.

The implications of this finding go beyond one species. Across the world's oceans, from the fog-draped shores of the Pacific Northwest to the wild swells of Tasmania, kelp forests are indeed vanishing–but their own cells might hold the blueprints for their survival. "All kelps share the same life cycle," Gonzalez says, so this knowledge–of heat-hardened lineages and stress-tested spores–could ripple outward. With each discovery, scientists edge closer to restoring these forests not just in one sea but in many, coaxing back the submerged canopies that breathe life into the planet's shifting currents.

About the Author

Avery Schuyler Nunn is an avid surfer, free diver and environmental science journalist based in California. She earned her Master of Science degree from Columbia University in 2021 and has used her notebook and camera as tools for exploration, both above and beneath the surface, ever since. She is a freelance contributor to Scientific American, National Geographic, Smithsonian Magazine, *Grist, and more. Follow her work on Instagram and X (formerly Twitter) @ earthyave and at www.averyschuylernunn.com*

Science in Depth--Mini Subs Unlock Mysteries Deep Below the Ocean's Surface

By Emily Anthes

Deep under the ocean's surface lies a treasure trove of new life forms, fuel sources and knowledge. But, given the darkness, freezing temperatures and crushing pressure, it's not easy to get there. Indeed 95 percent of the ocean remains unexplored; we know more about the surface of Mars than we do about the seafloor. "More than half of the planet is covered by water more than 3,000 meters [two miles] deep," says Chris German, chief scientist for the deep submergence group at the Woods Hole Oceanographic Institution in Cape Cod, Mass. "Most of the life that exists on the planet exists in the oceans. But we know so little about it."

That is beginning to change, as engineers and scientists create new submersible vehicles and probes capable of making the deep blue yonder more accessible than ever. By the 1970s, there were several small submersibles capable of taking people into the deep ocean (generally considered to be water deeper than two miles). Today, several nations–including the U.S., Russia, Japan and France–have built their own human-occupied vehicles (HOVs) and use them for scientific research.

"Humans are by most measures kind of the best in situ sensor you can get," says Andy Bowen, the lead engineer for several Woods Hole deep ocean vehicles. "The human eye and the other senses can learn things about the environment more quickly than almost any other technology." Because they have human operators on board, the systems are also easily maneuverable and can range freely, without having to stay alongside a vessel at the surface. But manned vehicles have some definite drawbacks. They're big, heavy and expensive–the newest human occupied vehicle, currently being designed for Woods Hole, has been forecast to cost $50 million–so only a handful of them have been built. There aren't nearly enough of them to carry out all the studies that scientists are interested in conducting in the deep sea.

Robotic submersibles—or ROVs, for remotely operated vehicles—are typically tethered to a ship on the surface of the water, where human operators control their movements. The machines also often carry a variety of sensors and cameras, transmitting data and images back to the surface vessel. ROVs can spend weeks, or even months, at a time underwater. (HOVs, on the other hand, can only support human life for a few days on the seafloor before having to resurface.)

HOVs and ROVs will continue to see incremental improvements, but the real advances will come in engineering so-called autonomous underwater vehicles (or AUVs), which combine the best of both worlds, Bowen says. AUVs are robotic vehicles that need no human intervention—they not only swim untethered, independent of a ship, but also are self-piloting, thanks to onboard software and sensors. "As our abilities to control or promote autonomy improve, and the behaviors that these robots have continue to become more complex," Bowen says, "it's quite possible that most of the exploration of the ocean will be done by autonomous vehicles."

The work scientists hope to undertake in coming years could lead to powerful new medicines (courtesy of some of the strange, undiscovered creatures of the deep), provide important information about climate change, and yield clues to natural disasters like tsunamis and earthquakes. German says, "It's not safe to ignore the ocean if you want to understand the planet."

Section 2: Indigenous Lands

2.1 Indigenous Lands Ace Biodiversity Measurements
By Jason G. Goldman

2.2 Indigenous Amazon Communities Fight Deforestation with New Early-Alert Tool
By Annie Sneed

2.3 Great Nicobar Island Is a Paradise in Danger
By Madhusree Mukerjee

Indigenous Lands Ace Biodiversity Measurements

By Jason G. Goldman

Scientists, conservation organizations and governments trying to stem the tide of extinction often focus efforts on protected areas such as national parks and wildlife preserves. But with as many as a million species at risk, this strategy may not be enough to conserve wildlife, especially in a world increasingly disrupted by climate change.

Slowing the mass extinction that now appears to be underway will require more creative means of coexisting alongside wild plants and animals. A new study underscores the effectiveness of some such approaches by examining indigenous-managed lands.

"We show really strongly that, from a biodiversity standpoint in terms of species richness, indigenous-managed lands are at least comparable to protected areas," says biologist Richard Schuster of Carleton University. And in some places, they far surpass parks and preserves—even though indigenous communities may utilize their lands' resources by hunting or foraging for food.

Schuster and his team analyzed more than 15,000 areas in Australia, Brazil and Canada. They found that the total diversity of birds, mammals, amphibians and reptiles was highest on lands either managed or co-managed by indigenous groups, whereas randomly selected locations with no formal protection were the least biodiverse. For threatened species in particular, indigenous lands scored slightly higher than protected lands on overall species richness in Brazil and Canada, as well as higher for threatened amphibians and reptiles in Australia, mammals in Brazil, and birds and reptiles in Canada. The results were published last November in *Environmental Science and Policy*.

Each country has a different geography, climate and colonization history. Yet remarkably, Schuster says, the best indicator for species diversity is whether a given area was managed by an indigenous community. He points out that practices such as sustainable hunting, fishing and foraging, as well as prescribed burning, are more likely to occur in such areas. Don Hankins, an ecologist at California State University, Chico, who is a member of the Plains Miwok indigenous nation and was not involved in the study, agrees. "There's probably going to be more of a connection to the land," he says, "and a use of the land for the things that are there, compared to a national park."

"It's really important to listen to the people who live on the land and have them drive the stewardship efforts going forward," Schuster says, adding that partnering with indigenous communities may enable the world's countries to better meet a wide range of conservation goals: "We really need all the help we can get as a global community to avert the extinction crisis that we're facing right now."

About the Author

Jason G. Goldman is a science journalist based in Los Angeles. He has written about animal behavior, wildlife biology, conservation, and ecology for Scientific American, Los Angeles *magazine, the* Washington Post, *the* Guardian, *the BBC,* Conservation *magazine, and elsewhere. He contributes to* Scientific American's *"60-Second Science" podcast, and is co-editor of* Science Blogging: The Essential Guide *(Yale University Press). He enjoys sharing his wildlife knowledge on television and on the radio, and often speaks to the public about wildlife and science communication.*

Indigenous Amazon Communities Fight Deforestation with New Early-Alert Tool

By Annie Sneed

Efforts to preserve the Amazon rain forest, which supports immense biodiversity and locks away about 123 billion metric tons of climate-threatening carbon, are growing ever more urgent as the ecosystem's destruction accelerates. Indigenous peoples have been trying to protect the region by patrolling their territorial boundaries for illegal activities, blocking dam construction, and more. But rapid deforestation continues.

A recent study shows that combining on-the-ground monitoring with satellite data and smartphone technology could help put the brakes on Amazon deforestation–and potentially that of forests elsewhere. The results were detailed in the *Proceedings of the National Academy of Sciences USA*.

Illegal logging, agriculture and coca cultivation particularly threaten the Amazon in the Peruvian Indigenous communities the study examined–and outsiders are often the culprits. The research team wondered if providing training for local people to use satellite-based "early deforestation alerts" could help.

The scientists collaborated with 76 Indigenous communities, 36 of which participated in using these alerts to watch over the forest. Three people from each of the latter communities received training to use an early-alert system on a smartphone app and to patrol forests and document damage.

Over the next two years these trained participants were paid to work as forest monitors and received monthly alerts via the app when satellite data indicated local forest losses. Monitors investigated alerts and patrolled for deforestation in other areas. They reported confirmed losses back to their communities, which decided whether to deal with the culprits on their own or inform state authorities.

The researchers analyzed the same forest-loss satellite data from the given time period in all 76 communities. They found the early-alert program reduced forest loss by 8.4 hectares in the first year–a 52 percent reduction compared with the average loss in the control communities, says study co-author Tara Slough, a political economist at New York University. "This reduction in deforestation was concentrated in communities facing the largest threat" of forest loss, she adds. "If one were to continue the program, targeting it to the communities facing the biggest threats should avert the most tree-cover loss."

Results for the monitoring program were less striking in its second year, when forest loss was reduced by only 3.3 hectares compared with that in control communities. The researchers suggest a Peruvian government campaign against coca cultivation that year may have discouraged deforestation in both experimental and control communities' territories, shrinking differences between the two groups in the pilot program.

Experts say this approach to tackling Amazonian deforestation–community monitoring combined with smartphone early alerts–looks promising. "Would this work in all communities that have high risk of deforestation? Given the results, it's worth a try," says Catherine Tucker, a forest governance researcher at the University of Florida, who was not involved in the study. But some communities may not have access to the resources needed for such a program, or their territories may hold valuable minerals or petroleum that would increase the risk of deforestation by outsiders despite monitoring efforts, Tucker notes.

Indigenous groups may continue the work they started in the pilot program. "We want to replicate this in other communities. In doing so, we are making a contribution to the world," wrote Francisco Hernandez Cayetano, a community member involved in the research and president of the Federation of the Ticuna and Yaguas Communities of the Lower Amazon, in a translated statement to *Scientific American*. "We as Indigenous peoples ask the world for support."

About the Author

Annie Sneed is a science journalist who has written for the New York Times, Wired, *Public Radio International and* Fast Company.

Great Nicobar Island Is a Paradise in Danger

By Madhusree Mukerjee

In 1667 a Swedish sailor reported that on his travels in the Far East he'd landed on the island of Great Nicobar, whose inhabitants had "a tail hanging like a cat's tail, but bald, and they could toss it however they liked, like a cat does." He'd evidently encountered the Shompen, who tie a strip of bark around the waist, letting its end dangle behind them. More than a century later this fanciful account led Scottish philosopher Lord Monboddo to postulate that the islanders were the common ancestors of humans and orangutans (both of which had lost their tails).

Science has since learned more about evolution, but the Shompen remain almost as enigmatic as ever. Numbering anywhere between 200 and 400, these hunters, gatherers and shifting cultivators mostly live in the steep, forested interior of Great Nicobar and shun outsiders. Only fragments of their language, culture and beliefs have been deciphered by academics. This past April seven Shompen men who had emerged from the forest were persuaded to cast ballots in India's general elections—although they can have little idea what a nation of 1.4 billion people is, let alone what elections are. Nor may they comprehend the danger they are in. As 39 scholars warned in February, the Shompen are facing "a death sentence" that is "tantamount to the international crime of genocide."

The Indian government, which inherited Great Nicobar Island from British colonizers, is about to build a massive transshipment terminal there. Described as a new Hong Kong, the $9-billion free-trade zone is to include a port with an eventual capacity to handle 16 million cargo containers a year, a town for 350,000 people resettled from mainland India, ancillary industries, a power plant and an international airport to be used by 4,000 peak-hour passengers.

The project will fell close to a million primeval rainforest trees in its initial phase alone and ultimately spread over 244 square kilometers—nearly a fifth of Great Nicobar. It's not only the Shompen who will be devastated. The island is also home to the Great Nicobarese, an Indigenous people who lived mainly along the southern and western coast until the massive tsunami of 2004 washed most of them away. The survivors were evacuated to the eastern coast, where they reunited with compatriots who returned from studying or visiting elsewhere. The Great Nicobarese have long pleaded with the Indian government to be allowed to return to their ancestral lands. But these are to be subsumed by facilities associated with the complex.

Just as worrisome, this emerald drop in an ink-blue ocean, one of the most pristine places left on Earth, is "globally irreplaceable from a biodiversity conservation viewpoint," according to the Alliance for Zero Extinction. The silver-sand beach edging Galathea Bay, at the southern end of Great Nicobar, for example, is the Northern Indian Ocean's largest nesting site for endangered Leatherback sea turtles, a species so venerable that it's shared Earth not only with us but also with the dinosaurs. This exquisite bay, which contains at least 117 species of corals, is to be dredged and developed into the container terminal, a seawall almost entirely blocking its entrance—a death trap for marine animals.

Great Nicobar is a also a UNESCO biosphere reserve and part of the Sundaland biodiversity hotspot, a region whose extraordinary biodiversity inspired the evolution theory of Alfred Russel Wallace, Charles Darwin's great rival. Of the more than 2,500 species of fauna and flora thus far documented on the island, 17 percent are endemic—found only on Great Nicobar or sometimes also on the other, far smaller, islands of the Nicobar archipelago.

Environmentalists have warned that the clear-cutting, blasting, dredging, construction, dumping of debris, ship traffic, pollution of multiple kinds and the enormous influx of outsiders with their animals and germs will devastate the Indigenous people and the creatures who live on and around Great Nicobar. No matter: after Prime Minister Narendra Modi announced the project in August 2020, his government shepherded it past all regulatory and legal hurdles, in such haste that it repeatedly tripped over itself.

In January 2021, for instance, India's minister of environment, forest and climate change released a document listing Galathea Bay among the most important marine turtle habitats in India–apparently unaware that a wildlife board, which he also headed, had days earlier revoked the bay's protected status. All that happened long before a private firm with no experience in conservation published an omission-ridden draft of an environmental impact assessment (EIA) in December 2021. Among other things, the EIA failed to mention all but two of the 15 species of dolphins and whales spotted in waters near Great Nicobar.

The sequence of events indicates that the Modi government selected Galathea Bay as the project site with no consideration of how it might affect either Indigenous people or wildlife. Nor does it seem keen to understand the full impact. Government-affiliated scientists seem to still have access to Great Nicobar, but for independent researchers, obtaining permits to work on the island has become like "getting a ticket to the moon," one observer says. Earlier this year a senior official entrusted with protecting Indigenous rights blasted the project's critics as being part of "an international conspiracy."

I'm no conspirator; I'm just in love with this part of the world. Two decades ago I wrote a book about the hunter-gatherers of the Andaman archipelago, which lies north of the Nicobar Islands. (A few of the Andaman islanders enforced their voluntary isolation, essential for their survival, by killing an American missionary in 2018.) Great Nicobar has always been less accessible than the Andamans, except to Indian government officials and former defense personnel and their families, who were granted land parcels around Campbell Bay on the east coast, mainly in the 1970s. The Indian navy built an air station near the bay in 2012.

I've never visited the Nicobars. But over the years, as I heard tales of the elusive Shompen and of the island's strange birds and animals, I came to think of Great Nicobar as a magical world rather like Pandora of the *Avatar* movies–complete with Indigenous peoples, luminous mushrooms, majestic trees thousands of years old, and mysterious creatures of the forest, coastline and deep. To me, the "development" planned for this island is as much of a desecration as the invasion of Pandora.

The Andaman and Nicobar island chains are peaks of an undersea mountain range scraped off the ocean floor over millions of years as the Indian geological plate pushes under the Eurasian. As small green havens in a vast ocean, they're already a marine and aerial hub–with Great Nicobar being particularly significant.

Migratory birds using two great flyways, the Central Asian and the East Asian-Australasian, throng the island's shores and wetlands. And tracking by ecologist Kartik Shanker and his team indicates that every year thousands of Leatherback hatchlings travel from beaches on the Andaman and Nicobar Islands across the Indian Ocean, either 10,000 kilometers west to Madagascar and Mozambique or east to Indonesia and Australia. Decades later, as adults weighing up to a metric ton, the Leatherbacks return to their natal beaches to lay their own eggs. Human ecologist Manish Chandi has described as "supernatural" the spectacle of these leviathans hauling themselves out of the sea on a winter night to continue a cycle of life honed over millions of years.

Great Nicobar's surrounding waters have been only partially explored by naturalists. They contain some of the most pristine coral reefs in the world, with 273 documented species of stony corals, among which live, along the eastern coast alone, 256 species of fish. The coral reefs, sea grass beds, and craggy undersea ridges and valleys, sloping into inky depths on either side of the island chain, shelter and nourish "an incredible diversity" of marine mammals, says marine biologist Mahi Mankeshwar. Apart from the dugong, a manatee sibling and a distant relative of elephants, these include the Indo-Pacific bottlenose, Spinner, Pantropical Spotted, Risso's and Fraser's dolphins, orcas and false killer whales, Omura's whales and the enigmatic sperm whale.

Almost nothing is known about the region's sperm whales. But in other parts of the world, close-knit pods of female sperm whales and their offspring live mainly in tropical waters, communicating via clicks so structurally complex as to suggest a language. Different pods may even have different dialects. Young males leave their maternal pods to form "bachelor schools," gradually migrating toward the poles and becoming more solitary. As adults, they roam freezing polar waters or travel thousands of kilometers to tropical seas to seek females, spreading their genes around the globe.

What will the transshipment project do to aerial and marine visitors to Great Nicobar and its surrounding seas? Conservationists' detailed critique of the EIA offers a clue. The star of the East Asian-Australasian flyway, the Bar-tailed Godwit, can fly nonstop for more than 13,000 kilometers. But most migratory birds need frequent stops for nourishment, and, according to ornithologist Shashank Dalvi, coastal development in China has already destroyed many feeding grounds. Some species may not survive the loss of yet another link in this vital chain or the likely oil spills.

Shanker holds that Leatherback turtles are savvy enough to stay away from Galathea Bay if they sense disturbances there. That may spare most of them from collisions with ships, but they'd lose an idyllic nesting beach, places that are increasingly hard to come by. The species is already endangered by multiple other threats, such as drowning in fishing nets and climate change.

Coral reefs in Galathea Bay, home to myriads of weird and wonderful creatures, will be destroyed, and those for kilometers around will be smothered by silt or harmed by turbidity and water pollution. Bottlenose dolphins, often seen in the bay, and Omura's whales—two species that live in coastal waters—will lose their habitats. As for the other species of dolphins and whales in surrounding seas, described as "one of the last reserves of undisturbed marine mammal populations in the world," their survival will be threatened by, to name just a few factors, collisions with ships, undersea noise and oil spills.

One would think the aerial and marine visitors to Great Nicobar and its shores would alone preclude major development. But the creatures and plants native to the island, most of which evolved in isolation to yield a cornucopia of unique species, are just as intriguing—and so varied that entire books have been devoted to describing them.

Great Nicobar's endemic mammals include characters such as the Nicobar Long-tailed Macaque. Around 1900 these monkeys encountered a white explorer and aggravated him by throwing their hands on their face with "an expression of absolute horror," among other gestures "indicative of shocked and outraged feelings." Masters of tool use, these primates extract fibers from leaves to floss their teeth, scratch their backs with twigs and break open coconuts with rocks. So ingenious are they that, when raiding settlers' farms and orchards (which, to be fair, occupy land cleared of pandanus groves that the macaques used to feed on), they avoid attention by breaking up into small groups, each of which snacks discreetly on a different type of fruit or vegetable.

Then there are Nicobar Treeshrews, sentinels of the forest that, in the words of zoologist Louise Emmons, "border on the neurotic," squeaking maddeningly whenever they spot an intruder—and outing naturalists trying to hide in painstakingly camouflaged hideouts. So skittish are they that, fearing a predator might follow them to their nest, they feed their young for only a few minutes every two or three days.

Another endemic mammal, the Nicobar Flying Fox, is one of the world's only two known species of *Pteropus* fruit bats that is solitary in its roosting habits. According to a Great Nicobarese legend, an old lady was feeling cold and sick, so someone offered her a blanket. Eventually she got better and the weather got warmer, but by then the blanket was stuck to her back. Feeling unattractive in it, she began to venture out only at night, when no one else could see her. To this day, she roams the forest every night as a bat and protects it.

Great Nicobar is also classified as an important bird area in categories A1, "known or thought regularly to hold significant numbers of a globally threatened species," and A2, "known or thought to hold a significant population of at least two range-restricted species." Among the birds, the Great Nicobar Serpent Eagle (the world's smallest eagle), the Nicobar Jungle Flycatcher, the Nicobar Scops Owl and the Nicobar Parakeet live only on Great Nicobar or its small sibling, Little Nicobar. The iridescent Nicobar pigeon, a zoo favorite, is a relative of the dodo.

The idiosyncratic Nicobar Megapode lives as mating couples in forests near the coast, building mounds of sand, corals and plant debris to lay their eggs in. The rotting vegetation provides warmth to incubate the eggs; the female periodically checks the temperature with her feet to make sure it's optimal. Once the chicks have dug their way out of the mound, the couple spruces it up for the next brood. At least 50 of the 95 permanent nesting sites will be subsumed by the transshipment complex.

I won't start with the freshwater fish, reptiles, amphibians, insects and other arthropods and plants that are unique to Great Nicobar–the list is too long. One exception to note is that, curiously for a tropical island, Great Nicobar has no poisonous snakes. (But there is a type of reticulated python, which the Shompen eat.) Another is that the world's largest land crab lives here, too; it climbs coconut trees, nips off coconuts, retrieves them on the ground and cracks them open to eat the white flesh. And the Andaman water monitor somehow found its way here–but skipped the northern and central Nicobar islands.

Many of these creatures could be exterminated by the project. One of its most destructive aspects is the enormous influx of outsiders. On the Andaman Islands, for example, newcomers cleared forests for settlement, reducing humidity and precipitation and causing water shortages that have also plagued them. Along with them came animals like dogs and cats that prey on vulnerable creatures like sea turtles and nesting birds. Another danger is disease transmission: avian cholera killed many domestic fowl in the Campbell Bay settlement in 1997, birdwatcher Uday Mondal noted in an article, and some megapodes also seemed to be affected. But there is no record of how the megapodes fared.

A related problem is garbage. Dumping from the Campbell Bay settlement, with its population of about 6,000 (as measured in 2011), is already causing problems for locals. Having lost their former feeding grounds to urbanization, and with some of the settlers shooting, poisoning or electrocuting them to deter raids on plantations, the macaques sometimes feed on trash; they could get sick. The EIA describes the macaques as a "menace." If that's how the designated protectors of wildlife see these primates, which the International Union for Conservation of Nature classifies as "vulnerable," the chances of the Nicobar long-tailed macaque surviving alongside hundreds of thousands of settlers is slim.

In sum, the creatures that can will flee to the mountains, where they will displace others; those that can't will die. With its interior forests and streams still largely unexplored, chances are this wildlife paradise has many treasures that could be destroyed before they are documented. Every zoological or botanical expedition finds new species, including, this past January, an endemic flowering plant.

"We've barely scratched the surface," Chandi says.

Of all Great Nicobar's inhabitants, the most enigmatic may be our fellow humans, the Shompen. Steep hills, dense jungles and malaria have defeated most adventurers who have sought to visit their interior settlements. Still, the tales these travelers brought back, as well as accounts collected with the help of the Great Nicobarese, offer a rough sense of how the Shompen live.

They spear crocodiles, fish, and other animals and gather fruit and other edibles. Curiously (and unlike the Andaman islanders), the Shompen don't use bows and arrows. Only partly nomadic, they build huts on platforms, usually near pandanus groves, which in turn are found near streams. They tend to the groves and, in small patches, cultivate tubers and vegetables.

A few Shompen men, possibly from different groups within the forest, traditionally visited the coastal Great Nicobarese villages to exchange jungle produce such as cane and honey for iron tools, tobacco, cloth and other goods. The coast dwellers, in turn, acknowledged Shompen guardianship of the jungle by, for example, seeking their permission before cutting a tree there, anthropologist Ajay Saini has noted.

Decades back, when the Indian government cleared space for settlers near Campbell Bay, it cut down pandanus groves that the Shompen had nurtured and displaced several of their hamlets. Nowadays the authorities offer the shifting cultivators rations of rice and lentils, which, again, a handful of men arrive to collect. But the Shompen refuse to allow outsiders to follow them back into the jungle. At some point, "they stop and stay put until we move away, or they just pack up their belongings and disappear" into the forest, Chandi relates.

So impenetrable is the terrain that each Shompen band, consisting of a handful of families, is isolated enough to possess its own dialect. Linguist George van Driem reviewed compilations of Shompen words to conclude that their language, like those of the Nicobarese, belongs to the Mon-Khmer branch of the Austroasiatic family, spoken mainly in Vietnam and Cambodia. Genetic studies support this view, while adding detail. They show that the Shompen and the Nicobarese descend from the same founding population originating in Southeast Asia. Unlike the Nicobarese, however, the Shompen have been genetically isolated for about 14,000 years, except for an influx of Y chromosomes–that is, male DNA–about 3,000 years ago.

Genes say little about geography, geneticist T. Sitalaximi cautions, but it seems reasonable to infer that the Shompen's ancestors were isolated since arriving on Great Nicobar about 14,000 years ago. The men who merged with them 3,000 years ago were closely related to the Indigenous Aeta of the Philippines and the Semang and Orang Asli of Malaysia, according to Sitalaximi–peoples whom earlier scholars had mistakenly, it seems, linked with the Andamanese.

Although the Shompen are understandably wary of outsiders, the Nicobarese have traditionally welcomed them. Before the 2004 tsunami, they lived in peaceful beachside villages, crafting canoes to travel to nearby islands and to fish in the coral reefs. They raised pigs, grew vegetables and nurtured coconut groves. Ancient seafarers traveling along trade routes between China and India, or even as far west as the Roman Empire, routinely stopped on the Nicobar Islands to stock up with coconuts and other supplies.

Around 1292 Marco Polo landed on one of the islands, possibly Great Nicobar, and later reported that the people possessed magnificent lengths of colored silk, which they bought from passing merchants. They didn't use the cloths to adorn themselves–they were naked–but kept the sashes "hung over rails in their houses as a token of wealth and magnificence." Their island was munificent: its "noble trees of great worth" included "red sandal, coconuts (which among us are called Pharoah's nuts), apples of paradise, cloves, brazil, and many other good trees."

I've never visited the Nicobars, but I, too, have been graced by Nicobarese hospitality. One blistering afternoon in May 1998, I was returning from a visit to a beachside settlement of Onge, the Indigenous people of Little Andaman Island. The path was sandy, so I kept falling off my man-sized rented bicycle; the rainforest's canopy trees had been felled by a government-owned corporation, so the sun blazed down; and my water supply had run out. I was utterly drained by the time I dragged my bike into a Nicobarese village on the way back. A young woman standing by one of the elevated huts beckoned to me; with a single stroke, she sliced open a coconut and offered it. "I drank gratefully of the cool water, sugar and salt," I wrote in my book—all that I needed to be on my way.

On December 26, 2004, when the tsunami hit, it washed away all but nine of the Great Nicobarese who were living on the western coast. Among the survivors were Mathias, his girlfriend and his brother, who were in a canoe at sea, rowing back home after having spent Christmas night partying at another village. Thrown onto the island by the waves, they found everything destroyed. Wretched and hungry, they trekked uphill to the nearest Shompen settlement, which was unscathed. The forest dwellers gave the brothers a knife and a pair of fire-making sticks. Over the next week, the trio met up with six other survivors. The implements gifted by the Shompen enabled the five men and four women to hold out for 35 days on turtle eggs and wild boar until Chandi and others arrived in search of survivors.

Mathias now serves as an interpreter, translating between Hindi and Shompen. It was through him that anthropologist Vishvajit Pandya asked a Shompen man what he thought about development. "If you must cut the jungle, cut it along the coast. Do not come near our hills," the man replied forcefully. "Do not climb our hills."

But the power plant and airport the Indian government plans to construct will consume two or three Shompen hamlets near the Galathea River, which drains into its namesake bay, as well as two wetlands teeming with waterbirds and saltwater crocodiles, where the Shompen hunt and forage. The displaced bands will be forced to move upstream, sparking competition for resources and conflict with other Shompen groups, Chandi worries. The effluents from the power plant will most likely poison the surrounding soil and the river, where the Shompen fish and collect drinking water.

The forest dwellers will also, and inevitably, encounter construction workers and other outsiders, probably with dire consequences. Sexual violence committed by settlers has been a serious problem on the Andamans and could become one on the Nicobars as well. Worse, having lived largely in isolation, the Shompen have little immunity to the diseases that thrive in the outside world and could be devastated by epidemics, as happened with the Andaman islanders. Whatever microbe killed nearly 100 Shompen in the 1980s of diarrhea probably originated with the Campbell Bay settlement; more epidemics are inevitable.

The Great Nicobarese are less susceptible to infections but suffer from a multitude of ailments, such as heart disease and diabetes, because of altered diet and lifestyle since having been evacuated to Campbell Bay. They have long pleaded with authorities to be allowed to return to their former villages. But this section of the southwestern coast is earmarked for tourism and other facilities. "We feel helpless and abandoned and are extremely anxious about our future," the tribal council wrote to the chief administrator of the Andaman and Nicobar Islands in August 2022.

After news of the Great Nicobar project broke, Indian civil society launched a passionate and deeply informed campaign to save the island. Partly in response to its concerns and to meet regulatory requirements, the Indian government has announced mitigation measures that range from the ridiculous to the outrageous. The damage to Great Nicobar's millions-year-old rainforest is to be compensated for by afforestation on dry hills of western India, which has a completely different ecology and will do nothing to save the island's species. And whatever Shompen territory survives is to be protected from poachers by erecting a "state of [the] art Geo fencing solution equipped with Optical/Thermal cameras, Satellite Phones, Drones"–a militarized border that will terrorize the Indigenous people into staying away from their own spaces.

Yet another response is to set up new wildlife sanctuaries on three small islands off the northern coast of Great Nicobar. That might seem like a good idea—but the devil is in the details. Meroe Island is to be a coral sanctuary, although its coral diversity is unknown. Menchal Island is now a megapode sanctuary, but it has two pairs of megapodes at most and cannot compensate for the loss of Great Nicobar's megapode population. Three beaches on Little Nicobar will be a Leatherback sanctuary. Leatherbacks already nest on a few of Little Andaman's beaches—which are too small to host the roughly 1,000 females that will be displaced from Galathea.

Bizarrely, these three islands will now be off-limits to the Great and Little Nicobarese, who have traditionally used and protected them. "Our customs and practices have ensured the integrity of all life on these islands," they protested in a letter to Indian authorities. Menchal, for instance, is guarded by a spirit named Pingaeyak, and Meroe is cared for by a community elder. Similarly, a hunting taboo protects dugongs near the seagrass beds to the north of Great Nicobar, where the highly endangered mammals feed. "That's why the dugongs still thrive there," Chandi says.

Given the Modi government's track record, the disregard for the environment and Indigenous rights implicit in this massive project is not surprising. What is remarkable is its impracticality. Take the matter of geology. Scientist and journalist Pankaj Sekhsaria has pointed out that the 9.1-magnitude earthquake of 2004 sank the southern tip of Great Nicobar by around four meters. Even without a tsunami, another major earthquake on this very active fault could destroy the township and kill hundreds of people.

Former army officer and senior administrator M. G. Devasahayam has further argued that a container terminal on Great Nicobar is "neither economically viable nor financially feasible." The enormous construction cost, most of which the Indian taxpayer is expected to bear, will take at least 50 years to pay off because the container terminal, which has no hinterland to absorb or export goods, will struggle to draw traffic away from established ports such as Colombo. (And that's assuming climate change hasn't done away with the global shipping industry by 2074.) India's shipping ministry, which revealingly advertises the project as a once in "a lifetime opportunity for investors to reap gold," had announced that, should the Modi-led Hindu nationalist alliance win the elections–which it has–the ministry would invite bids for the complex by July and begin construction by the end of the year.

I have listed, as objectively as I can, many reasons why this is not a good idea. I can also point out that the Global Safety Net, a blueprint to "solve the twin crises of biodiversity loss and climate change," lists the southern end of Great Nicobar, including Galathea Bay, among the areas requiring protection. I can note that six out of nine planetary boundaries have already been crossed, that tropical rainforests store humungous quantities of carbon, that heat waves aggravated by climate change have already killed hundreds of people this year, that deforestation can spread novel viruses that most people have no immunity to, or that no one knows just when biodiversity loss will reach a tipping point so that the entire web of life unravels.

I can rage: with birds and monkeys falling dead from trees, fish floating up in the millions, forests burning and corals bleaching because of overheated summers–how does it make sense to willfully destroy rainforest and reefs and mangroves and beaches with their myriad irreplaceable creatures? Or the rare cultures in which people know how to live in this world with love for other beings rather than contempt?

In truth, perhaps I care about this island, which I have never seen and probably will never see, because it reminds me that living on this Earth, so battered and yet still so beautiful, so full of mystery and magic, is a privilege. That we need to hold onto this magic, because without it life will be just a little bit less worth living.

About the Author

Madhusree Mukerjee was a senior editor at Scientific American, *where she covered psychology, anthropology, and diverse other topics. She has authored two nonfiction books:* Churchill's Secret War *(Basic Books, 2010) and* The Land of Naked People *(Houghton-Mifflin, 2003). She has a Ph.D. in physics from the University of Chicago and received a Guggenheim fellowship to complete her first book. She has written numerous articles on Indigenous issues, development, and colonialism and is working on a third book.*

Section 3: The Arctic

3.1 Arctic Exploitation May Harm Animals Large and Small
By Chiara Eisner

3.2 The Arctic Is in Dire Straits, 20 Years of Reporting Show
By Andrea Thompson

Arctic Exploitation May Harm Animals Large and Small

By Chiara Eisner

As sea ice in the Arctic Ocean dwindles with each successive year of rising global temperatures, it has become easier and more common for companies to venture into the region for fishing, shipping, and oil and gas exploration. Though the boats, rigs and other trappings of human activity have already quickly moved into this fragile environment, scientists are only just beginning to understand how the light, sound and chemical pollution they bring with them is impacting the Arctic's marine ecosystem.

Some researchers have started filling in the gaps, including two teams working in Norway that presented new findings about the behaviors of zooplankton and killer and humpback whales at the Arctic Frontiers 2020 conference in the nation's city of Tromsø in January. Though zooplankton may seem to have little in common with whales, research shows that creatures at both extremes of the Arctic food web are critical to the health of the marine ecosystem. Understanding how industry affects these animals could help inform policies governing commercial activities in the Arctic.

Light Sensitivity

Tiny zooplankton move in response to light cues during the day. When the sun rises in the morning, they drift down closer to the seabed to avoid predators. When the sun sets, they ascend toward the surface to feed. During the 24 hours of darkness occurring in the Arctic winter—a nearly month-long period called the polar night—scientists had thought zooplankton simply stopped moving under the sea ice, says Jørgen Berge, a taxonomist and marine biologist at UiT–the Arctic University of Norway.

But that thinking changed after the winter of 2007–2008, when Berge noticed that zooplankton in the fjords of the Svalbard archipelago were still moving up and down in patterns similar to the ones they followed when the sun shone. He found they could still sense and respond to low levels of light from the moon, the aurora borealis and background illumination from the sun—even under thick layers of ice and snow. "It was a complete surprise to us," Berge says.

In subsequent work, he showed that other Arctic denizens, such as shrimp, krill, herring and cod, would also respond to light levels that were orders of magnitude lower than the ones similar species experience in waters elsewhere around the world. This left him concerned that Arctic animals would be extra sensitive to artificial light and that exposure to it could change important aspects of their behavior. Such light pollution, which shines with an intensity and composition not found in nature, has been shown to disrupt the hormone production and metabolism of many vertebrate species, including fish—and humans.

To investigate, Berge monitored how Arctic animals moved in response to the artificial lights from just one ship: his own research vessel. In three locations during the polar night of 2019, Berge measured the total mass of the marine animals around the ship with the lights on and off. In each case, there was a significant difference. At one location, there were about half as many animals around the ship when the lights were switched on. In another, with a different animal population, the biomass increased with the lights on—a response Berge says is not surprising, because, like moths on land, some marine animals have adapted to be attracted to light instead of repelled by it.

This research, published Thursday in *Communications Biology*, has strong implications for the fishing industry, Berge says. Norwegian authorities currently gather information about the abundance of fish in the area throughout the year, including during the polar night, and use that information to determine fishing limits. But because these assessments are carried out with artificial lights on, "that could have a strong bias,"Berge notes. "Our ability to measure and understand and make good predictions as to how much you can fish could be based on wrong input data."

Likewise Berge believes that no scientific study that has ever been conducted during the polar night–with lights turned on–could be considered an unbiased representation of how the animals would naturally behave during that time. "In darkness and light, you will get two very different results, and the knowledge about the system will be very different," Berge says. Franz Hölker, an ecologist at the Leibniz Institute of Freshwater Ecology and Inland Fisheries in Germany, who studies light pollution but was not involved with the new work, agrees. He says Berge's findings mirror some of his own.

Safety concerns for humans make it impractical to ban artificial light in the Arctic altogether, Berge says. "Rather we need to understand what effects light pollution is causing." That way, the level of bias in scientific studies and fishery estimates could be quantified and, to some degree, corrected.

Where the Whales Are

The need for more knowledge of human industry's effects exists on the other end of the Arctic animal size scale as well. Though fishing, shipping, and oil and gas activities have expanded rapidly in the Arctic, "we have no idea what the whales are doing," says Evert Mul, a Ph.D. student at UiT. "We plan those activities without taking into account the presence and the distribution and the behavior of the whales."

To help change that situation, Mul and his colleagues at UiT and the Institute of Marine Research in Norway have tagged 45 killer whales and 30 humpback whales over the past seven years–many more than in previous tagging studies. Doing so allowed them to map how these whales interact with the human activities taking place in polar regions for what they say is the first time ever in this part of the Arctic.

Mul says the team's results, which he expects to publish this summer, show the whales spent significant amounts of time in the locations where there was heavy shipping traffic, as well as oil and gas installations. "And of course, they spend a lot of time near fishing vessels," because they are drawn to the massive amounts of fish the commercial boats collect, he says. It is not uncommon to see anywhere from 50 to 100 whales around a single vessel, Mul adds. Attracted to such a concentration of these spectacular animals, boats filled with tourists join the action, too.

Greg Breed, a biologist and associate professor at the University of Alaska Fairbanks, who was not involved with Mul's work, has observed similar confluences in human and whale activity during his own studies in the Canadian Arctic. "They happen to overlap because they're using the same space," he says. For example, whales take advantage of the ice-free passages cleared by large vessels.

Though the whales may seem to benefit from easy snacks swiped while swimming near fishing boats, human activity may harm the animals, too. Many of the cetaceans tagged in Mul's study have visible scars from entanglement with fishing nets or collisions with boat hulls or propellers. Noise pollution can interfere with the complex songs the creatures use to communicate, he says. Chemical pollution is another issue. Killer whales already have some of the highest contamination from polychlorinated biphenyls (PCBs) on earth, and modeling has demonstrated this problem could endanger the long-term survival of the Arctic killer whale population.

As Breed points out, though, it is also possible that stressors other than physical injuries or pollutants–such as interruptions to the marine food chain linked to warming ocean waters–could be having more of an impact on Arctic whale populations. Potential impacts, including those identified by Mul and Berge, should be considered when making decisions about industry in the Arctic, the researchers say. Like Berge, Mul believes the best course of action at this point is not to call for drastic bans but for policies that make obvious sense–such as better regulation of pollutants where whales are more abundant. Mul also stresses the need to continue improving the information scientists have about the magnitude of the problem.

Even with limited knowledge, those who are planning industrial activities in the Arctic still need to be aware of the possibility that their presence could have repercussions, Mul says. He would like industries to at least "have the seasonal whale distribution in the back of their mind, even while we are still continuing to understand, and to map, the situation." To help with this effort, Mul plans to hold a meeting with Norwegian industry leaders to inform them of his results and seek feedback about how he can present the information in a way that is useful to them. "It's very important," he says, "to have at least a basic understanding of what the animals are doing that we are going to share this region with."

About the Author

Chiara Eisner is a multimedia investigative journalist whose work has focused on international politics, criminal justice, and science and technology.

The Arctic Is in Dire Straits, 20 Years of Reporting Show

By Andrea Thompson

The Arctic is a dramatically different place than it was 20 years ago, when scientists first began giving it an annual checkup—and its current state is dire.

The first Arctic Report Card was released by the National Oceanic and Atmospheric Administration in 2006. Since then the region has warmed twice as fast as the global average. About 95 percent of the oldest, thickest sea ice is gone—the sliver that remains is collected in an area north of Greenland. Even the central Arctic Ocean is becoming warmer and saltier, causing more ice melt and changing how much heat is released into the atmosphere in a way that affects weather patterns around the world.

Those are just some of the stark changes 20 years have wrought. The findings were highlighted in the 2025 Arctic Report Card, released on Tuesday.

"The very first Arctic Report Card in 2006 was issued because things were changing rapidly, and this need for rapid updates was felt keenly," said Rick Thoman of the International Arctic Research Center at the University of Alaska Fairbanks during a press briefing at the annual meeting of the American Geophysical Union. "Every year does not have a new record, but cumulatively [the report] provides a record of where we've been and a guide—just a guide—to where we're going."

Between October 2024 and September 2025, surface air temperatures in the Arctic were at their warmest since at least 1900, according to the report. The 10 warmest years in the region have all fallen within the past decade.

In the ocean, the layer of sea ice that expands each winter as temperatures drop reached a record low annual peak. The summer minimum extent was the 10th lowest in at least 47 years. The disappearing sea ice means that less of the sun's rays are reflected back to space and are instead absorbed by the ocean, driving a vicious cycle of warming that, in turn, causes more ice loss. The dwindling sea ice also means critical habitats for iconic species such as polar bears and walrus are fast disappearing.

The Arctic Ocean is undergoing what scientists are calling "Atlantification"–a process where warm, salty water from the Atlantic flows north, changing how waters of different temperatures and densities are layered in the Arctic, disrupting ecosystems and altering how heat moves from the water to the air.

A warmer ocean also helped a powerful storm, former Typhoon Halong, maintain strength across the Pacific in October 2025, eventually barreling into Alaska with hurricane-force winds and devastating storm surge. More than 1,500 residents were evacuated, and some villages were all but destroyed.

Glaciers, too, are rapidly melting away, the report found. Glaciers in Alaska have lost 125 vertical feet since the mid-20th century. Greenland's ice sheet didn't lose as much ice this year as it did in some previous years. But it continued to pour meltwater into the oceans, raising sea levels.

The Arctic is simply becoming wetter, with more precipitation falling as rain instead of snow. June snow cover over the entire Arctic is half of what it was 60 years ago, the report found.

Permafrost also continues to thaw, releasing once trapped carbon into the atmosphere and disgorging iron and other elements that have turned rivers and streams orange. These "rusting rivers," found in more than 200 watersheds, are more acidic than normal and have elevated levels of toxic metals that endanger local ecosystems. And as the permafrost thaws, the tundra of the Arctic biome is shrinking, and the boreal forest biome is creeping northward, disrupting ecosystems.

About the Author

Andrea Thompson is senior desk editor for life science at Scientific American, covering the environment, energy and earth sciences. She has been covering these issues for nearly two decades. Prior to joining Scientific American, she was a senior writer covering climate science at Climate Central and a reporter and editor at Live Science, where she primarily covered earth science and the environment. She has moderated panels, including as part of the United Nations Sustainable Development Media Zone, and appeared in radio and television interviews on major networks. She holds a graduate degree in science, health and environmental reporting from New York University, as well as a B.S. and an M.S. in atmospheric chemistry from the Georgia Institute of Technology. Follow Thompson on Bluesky @andreatweather.bsky.social

Section 4: The Unknown

4.1 Out of Sight, 'Dark Fungi' Run the World from the Shadows
By Cody Cottier

4.2 Drones Sample Rare Specimens from Cliffs and Other Dangerous Places
By Susan Cosier

4.3 Under Soil and above Caves, a Warren of Hidden Life
By Jennifer Frazer

4.4 Volcano Erupts after Lying Dormant for 12,000 Years, Sending Scientists Scrambling
By Stephanie Pappas

4.5 Giant Volcano Rewrites the Story of Seafloor Formation
By William W. Sager

4.6 Meet the Magnificent Microbes of the Deep Unknown
By Jeffery DelViscio

4.7 Mangrove Trees Are on the Move, Taking the Tropics with Them
By Michael Adno

Out of Sight, 'Dark Fungi' Run the World from the Shadows

By Cody Cottier

Why This Matters: The land, water and air around us are chock-full of DNA fragments from fungi that mycologists can't link to known organisms. These slippery beings are so widespread scientists are calling them "dark fungi." It's a comparison to the equally elusive dark matter and dark energy that permeate the universe. Like those invisible entities, dark fungi are hidden movers and shakers, prime examples of what E. O. Wilson called "the little things that run the world."

If you want to discover a hidden world of new life-forms, you don't have to scour dark caves or slog through remote rainforests. Just look under your feet. When then-graduate student Anna Rosling went to northern Sweden to map the distribution of a particular root-loving fungus, she found something much more intriguing: Many of her root samples contained traces of DNA from unknown species. Weirder still, she never encountered a complete organism. When the field season ended, she had only isolated bits of raw genetic material. The fragments clearly belonged to the fungal kingdom, but they revealed little else. "I got obsessed," recalls Rosling, now a professor of evolutionary biology at Uppsala University in Sweden.

Since then mycologists have realized that such phantoms are everywhere. Point to a patch of dirt, a body of water, even the air you're breathing, and odds are that it is teeming with mushrooms, molds and yeasts (or their spores) that no one has ever seen. In ocean trenches, Tibetan glaciers and all habitats between, researchers are routinely detecting DNA from obscure fungi. By sequencing the snippets, they can tell they're dealing with new species, thousands of them, that are genetically distinct from any known to science. They just can't match that DNA to tangible organisms growing out in the world.

These slippery beings are so widespread that scientists are calling them "dark fungi." It's a comparison to the equally elusive dark matter and dark energy that make up 95 percent of our universe and exert tremendous influence on, well, everything. Like those invisible entities, dark fungi are hidden movers and shakers. Scientists are convinced they perform the same vital functions as known fungi, directing the flow of energy through ecosystems as they break down organic matter and recycle nutrients. Dark fungi are prime examples of what biologist E. O. Wilson called "the little things that run the world." But their cryptic lifestyle has made it a maddening challenge for scientists trying to show *how* exactly they run it.

Taxonomists have described just 150,000 of the millions of fungi predicted by global biodiversity estimates, and recent discoveries suggest a huge portion of what's left may be off-limits to routine biological investigation. "We have not even started to scratch the surface," says Henrik Nilsson, a mycologist at the University of Gothenburg in Sweden. "I'd be willing to bet that the clear majority will be dark." Given the central place of fungi in the web of life that sustains us, experts argue we should get a better grasp on them.

Everything we know about dark fungi comes from environmental DNA, or eDNA. That term refers to strings of base pairs–the building blocks of DNA that are constantly sloughing off all living things. Researchers can analyze these free-floating bits of double helix to determine which species have been hanging around an area without seeing them. To identify fungi specifically, scientists look to a handy genetic marker called the internal transcribed spacer (ITS), which consists of several hundred base pairs that evolve quickly and thus help distinguish between species. Although the ITS is only a tiny fraction of the genome, researchers can single it out and amplify it with the same polymerase chain reaction technology used in COVID lab tests. If an ITS sequence is different enough from all others in genetic databases, it is thought to represent a new species, whether scientists lay eyes on its physical form or not.

At the turn of the millennium, eDNA sequencing burst onto the scene as a new way to discover species. Scientists suddenly found themselves awash in a "flood of data," as David Hibbett, a mycologist at Clark University, and his colleagues wrote in 2009. That influx exposed the sheer vastness of dark fungi. Today, Hibbett says, "our understanding of the richness of fungal diversity is really being enlarged with these dark organisms."

Every year researchers stumble on some 2,000 new fungi via the standard route, spotting them in nature or under a microscope. Yet a single eDNA study can register 10 times more dark fungi than that. As often as not, the fragments are among the most abundant DNA samples in their ecosystem. "I don't think I ever saw an environmental sequencing study with less than 30 percent unknowns," Nilsson says, and the ratio is typically much higher. Sometimes only a minority of DNA sequences can be classified at any meaningful taxonomic level, narrowing them from a kingdom (in this case, fungi) to a phylum and then to a class, and so on down to a species.

Finding a full specimen can be difficult. Many fungi are microscopic, even unicellular, and a tiny sample of biological material may contain hundreds that are hard to isolate. Other species grow as visible mushrooms and rootlike mycelia, but they're ephemeral and therefore easy to miss. As for raising the organisms in a lab culture, it can be arduous to provide the right conditions. A team of Czech microbiologists recently claimed that "in theory, nothing is impossible to culture," but mycology is strapped for cash and personnel, so as a practical matter, our insight into dark fungi usually ends at DNA snippets.

What we do know isn't trivial, however. As Rosling put it, "In the environmental DNA sequence, there's so much more information than just the base pairs." By looking for similarities with known species, mycologists can pinpoint the closest relatives of a dark fungus, and from that they can often infer a lot about its life cycle and ecological role. Still, there's a limit to what someone can learn without a complete specimen, especially when there are no particularly close relatives. "If it's something out in left field," Hibbett says, "that's very mysterious."

Take the group of fungi whose DNA Rosling unearthed in grad school. Years later she was stunned to find one of them thriving in a long-forgotten culture from 1999. It turned out to be the first known member of a class called Archaeorhizomycetes, comprising hundreds of dark species that live in soils around the world. For reference, mammals are a class. "There are groups at that scale that we don't know," Rosling says with wonder.

In 2011 a British microbiologist named Meredith Jones discovered a possible new phylum, aptly named Cryptomycota, which was previously dark. (For reference, the class of mammals is a subgroup of the phylum Chordata.) Such discoveries are more than minor revisions to the tree of life. Besides adding an enormous branch on the fungal limb, Cryptomycota was a bombshell because it lacked the fibrous substance chitin, once considered a defining characteristic of all fungi. And since Rosling's team made its discovery, Archaeorhizomycetes have been deemed potential keystone species. If they weren't around–forming symbiotic relationships with plants, decomposing organic molecules into carbon and nitrogen that other organisms can utilize–whole ecosystems could collapse. Clearly we can't read the full story in DNA, but it's a starting point. Until researchers track down or culture dark fungi, they exist for us mainly as a great constellation of ITS sequences. Mycologists refer to those sequences as "barcodes" because they unambiguously link genetic material to a species. Of the 10 million barcodes in the worldwide DNA UNITE database, many are languishing under the label "unidentified."

Hoping to inspire interest in these taxonomic orphans, Nilsson made a list of the "top 50 most wanted fungi," representing the largest unidentified lineages for which there is DNA but no specimens. A couple have been defined, but he doesn't feel the rest have received enough attention since he put out the warrants in 2016. "Everyone wants to produce papers, and here's the chance," he says. "All the data have been assembled for you. Go and have a look, and I'm sure you can find something." Nilsson means one can do so not only digitally but also physically: UNITE entries include the geographic distribution of DNA sequences, so anyone can hunt for the corresponding species in the real world.

The list doesn't necessarily cover the most economically or ecologically significant dark fungi, just groups of them that have yet to be classified at even the highest levels of taxonomy, such as phylum and class. Nevertheless, when pressed for possible benefits, Nilsson has no trouble obliging. The unexplored edges of fungal biology could, for example, yield valuable chemicals or medicines (penicillin and the organ-rejection treatment cyclosporine are derived from fungi, to name just a couple). "One or more of these species will prove super important to humans," he says.

Most crucially, dark fungi are essential to the proper functioning of the biosphere. They're thoroughly entwined with the rest of nature. To preserve them and all the intricate, life-supporting processes they underlie, researchers have to keep pinning them down one by one. "Capturing that diversity," Rosling says, "can help us have a more informed perspective on conservation."

As techniques for handling eDNA advance, mycologists are better positioned than ever to extract the dark secrets. High-throughput sequencing and single-cell genomics—which, as the name implies, can glean nearly an entire genome from a single cell—both offer dramatic improvements over traditional barcode sequencing. Combined with cutting-edge technology for sorting and culturing the legion cells in environmental samples, such methods could give a deeper view into the enigmatic world of dark fungi. "Just imagine all the cool chemistry and biology and ecology that are going on," Nilsson says. "All these interactions, and we have absolutely no idea about them. That thought gives me energy."

About the Author

Cody Cottier is a freelance journalist based in Fort Collins, Colo.

Drones Sample Rare Specimens from Cliffs and Other Dangerous Places

By Susan Cosier

On a knife-edge ridge on Kauai, a delicate little plant with a tuft of yellow flowers sprouts from the rock. The only sounds are the wind, the murmur of waves far below—and the hum of drone propellers. The whine gets louder as another drone suspended from the first encloses the plant with two arms, a blade slicing through the stem. The device then gently lifts the plant, a member of the genus Schiedea, part of the carnation family. As the tiny specimen's leaves flutter in the air, the drone descends and delivers it directly to researchers waiting below.

This scene—repeated dozens of times with various plants on the Hawaiian island's tropical cliffsides as part of a new study—shows how drones can help scientists pluck rare and endangered plants from spots that would otherwise be dangerous, if not impossible, for humans to reach. Collecting samples is often necessary to better understand the plights of these species, and how to save them. "It's a fabulous development and use of technology to get a lot more information than a person trudging around," says Warren Wagner, a research botanist at the Smithsonian Institution. He was not part of the study but serves as a research associate at the National Tropical Botanical Garden, one of the institutions involved.

The study, published recently in *Nature Scientific Reports*, builds on decades of botanical investigations on Kauai, which has more than 250 native plant species. Historically, botanists have rappelled down the island's sheer rock faces to reach specific plants, going to extremes for samples that they can raise in a nursery to perpetuate species at risk of extinction. Ben Nyberg, a geographer and drone specialist at the National Tropical Botanical Garden, wanted to try using remote-controlled flying robots in places that are difficult to access.

Nyberg and his team used a commercially available drone to heft a separate robotic unit that they built from scratch and named the Mamba. When conceptualizing the device, the researchers had first tried to figure out how plant-picking arms could be made to reach out horizontally from a hovering drone itself. This idea quickly got complicated, says study co-author Guillaume Charron, an engineer from Outreach Robotics. "That's when we started brainstorming and we came up with the idea of suspending a remote-controlled robotic arm" on cables beneath a drone. Because the Mamba doesn't have to lift itself, an operator can use its propellers to keep it steady and maneuver it sideways precisely enough.

The Mamba's sampling components include a foam-padded grasping arm that can move like a wrist, and a hook that draws a plant's stem toward a blade. The team is now considering how to equip the Mamba with other tools, such as a vacuum that could suck in plant material or a nozzle that could spray a slurry of seeds and growing medium onto a cliffside for replanting.

Similar drone systems could help researchers reach other forbidding areas such as the tabletop mountains that jut above the Amazon jungle, or the sky islands (isolated mountain ranges rising abruptly from the desert) of the southwestern U.S. "The drone system could be used in a variety of additional applications like tree canopy studies, depositing and [data-collecting devices] in a range of environments, or even planting trees," says Nyberg, a study co-author who is completing a Ph.D. at the University of Copenhagen. "Basically, this allows users to reach completely inaccessible areas, wherever they may be."

The carnation species plucked from Kauai's high ridges appears to be a Schiedea never identified there before. Its seeds are now growing at the University of California, Irvine, with help from botanists Ann Sakai and Steve Weller–a married couple who have studied *Schiedea* for more than three decades and were impressed by the information gleaned from the drone's sampling. "They have been able to map in detail the population in a way that we could just never do by rappelling," Weller says. "I'm impressed, and I certainly think that it's a really nice new tool to be able to know more about these plants."

About the Author

Susan Cosier is a freelance journalist focused on science and the environment. She is based in Chicago. Follow Cosier on Twitter @susancosier

Under Soil and above Caves, a Warren of Hidden Life

By Jennifer Frazer

Most people who have heard of copepods – and there are precious few in this world – know them from the ocean, where they are a common member of the drifting life called plankton. They're little crustaceans, and more or less unremarkable looking. Here is one.

But copepods don't just live in the ocean. They also hide, like Gollum, in hidden pools and cavities in the Earth. These tiny cracks, crevices, and pockets of water are an invisible ecosystem teeming with life that humans can only imagine because we are far too large to ever visit them. The habitats are so small and varied that different rare species may live in labyrinths just yards from each other, but never meet.

Their home is called the epikarst, and it is a layer of Earth found in mostly limestone, dolomite, and gypsum rock between the dirt and any cave systems below, a layer called karst. It isn't quite soil and it isn't quite stone, and water that percolates through it may be captured or diverted in unexpected directions by fractures and liquid-filled cavities in the rock. This network of spaces can form a crazy quilt of habitats for a variety of different organisms. Most prominent is a bumper crop of small crustaceans, particularly our copepod friends. More on them later.

The diversity is high enough to rival that in the caves below, and the ecological niches either so unique or cut off by the geometry of rock within the epikarst as to form what are effectively islands of life, subject to the same evolutionary forces found on their much larger cousins in the ocean (an important field of biology called "Island biogeography", famously pioneered by Robert MacArthur and E.O. Wilson).

When water that has traveled through this micro-warren reaches any caves below, it drips out of the ceiling and may form quiet rimstone infinity pools bordered by ripply dams deposited by minerals that precipitate from the dripwater. They are usually serene, their glassy surfaces marred only by the occasional drop (which may accelerate to a proper shower after topside downpours).

When storms wash through this warren, the tiny animals that live there must hold on with everything they've got, in some cases resorting to structures including – I am not making this up – "anal teeth", for fear of being washed down into a place where they cannot survive.

Since we lack the sort of shrink rays regularly found in B-grade sci-fi films, none of us can visit the epikarst in person. We must rely on those unfortunates swept out of the rock by water and into caves below to tell us what might be living up there (which begs the question: what sorts of animals that are *really good* at clinging to cracks might be up there? And what hides in the layer below the karst?). As a result of our inability to thoroughly explore it, it is a great source of new species.

Such places include the rimstone pools of Conza Cave near Palermo, Sicily. Conza Cave is relatively small. Just 100 meters long, it slopes upward 20 meters from the entrance and contains five rimstone pools.

The rock matrix in which it formed is a mixture of limestone, dolomite, and biolitite. The cave is dead; that is, whatever hydrological forces acted to form it have ceased, and it no longer floods. The only water infiltration is through the drips from the ceiling into the rimstone pools. The pools are on top of boulders without an outlet, and are effectively sealed off from the rest of the cave by an impermeable calcite coating on their bottoms and edges, formed when the mineral precipitates from the percolation water. The pools, too, are thus islands – islands that periodically vanish.

The overburden – the layer of Earth between the ceiling and the surface – is also relatively thin at Conza Cave, measuring just 14 meters (46 feet). The water storage capacity of this layer is therefore small, and when the rains disappear in summer due to the Mediterranean climate, the drips drop off and the pools dry up through at least late spring and early summer, and sometimes also through the winter. Copepods do not have a resting stage capable of surviving dry conditions (unlike the tardigrades recently covered here). So any copepods washed out of the ceiling into the pools of this cave are doomed to die.

Some intrepid Italian caver-scientists from the University of Catania decided a few years ago to study what they found in these pools. They wanted to test whether the pools were colonized only by organisms dripping from the epikarst, and whether even though the layer is thin and rain is often scarce, that the epikarst above Conza Cave can be a permanent refuge for these organisms during hot dry weather. Since none of the pools were connected to each other, the five pools were also microsampling devices for gauging the biota of the epikarst above on a fine scale.

The spaces in the epikarst above must have retained some water throughout the year, as the scientists observed the copepods instantly reappeared in their pools with the onset of each rainy season and the re-formation of the pools.

What the scientists found over three years of monitoring those pools revealed something else amazing: three different copepod species consistently filled the same pools mere meters away from each other – two out of three of them new to science – indicating that in the rock above the ceiling were atolls of life whose inhabitants never seemed to mingle.

Subterranean copepods also tend to share certain features. They have extended reproductive periods, to maximize the chance of partners running into one another at receptive times. That held true for *B. stillae* in this study – invidividuals in all life stages were found throughout the entire sampling period. Such copepods also tend to produce just a few large eggs, an adaption to "adversity" found in species in many habitats. *B. stillae* had just five or six eggs per female, and they were the largest diameter ever recorded for its genus.

Such creatures also tend to have evolved special methods for clinging to their cracks, to avoid being swept too deep with the inexorable pull of water. In the case of *B. stillae*, this includes a long body with short, stout limbs bristling with little spines. It even includes a few teeth on their "anal operculum", a covering for the area in question. You can see three of them on the image at right above at the base of the copepod's body, between the two long spines. It's not "Hold on to your butt," – it's "Hold on *with* your butt". These little guys – like all inhabitants of the epikarst – are literally holding on for their dear lives with everything they've got.

The pools were roughly divided into two groups. Rimstone pools 4 and 5 consistently contained *Parastenocaris diversitatis*, a new species. The two pools were only 7 meters apart. Pools 1 and 3, about 10 meters apart, contained *Bryocamptus stillae* and *Speocyclops italicus*, and in one instance, pool 1 contained both. The two groups of pools were separated by 10-16 meters.

Pool No. 2 contained no copepods at all. The water that fed it must have come from a copepod desert, or from a fracture system where the copepods were easily able to prevent themselves from falling from the ceiling.

The authors suggest that there are two separate percolation units feeding the two groups of pools, perhaps divided by microfractures of different sizes or other characteristics that favor certain species over others. *P. diversitatis*, for example, is skinnier than *B. stillae*, and was found much less often in the pools. That may be because it can wedge itself into much tighter cracks than *B. stillae*, which also reduces the chances it will wash out of the ceiling.

Many other organisms were found in the pools besides copepods. The scientists also saw 12 tardigrades (water bears); 249 nematodes (roundworms); perhaps not surprisingly, 72 earthworms; and two mites. They also saw 102 albino ostracods – the same group of organisms that produces the firefly-like displays that so mesmerized me in the Caribbean a few years ago – but only in Pool 1.

Finding copepods with such restricted distributions was not entirely unexpected. Subterranean copepod species had already been known to have distributions of just a few hundred meters, and the epikarst fauna to be divided into ecological "blocks" based on hyperlocal environmental conditions., Still, finding entirely separate groups within just meters of each other seems extraordinary to me. If you extrapolate this finding to the entire karst-bearing land surface of the planet, the potential diversity seems staggering. Imagine all the little animals that could be squirreled away in all the little cracks and crevices inside millions of square miles of land, tucked far from the probing gaze of science.

About the Author

Jennifer Frazer, an AAAS Science Journalism Award–winning science writer, authored The Artful Amoeba blog for Scientific American. She has degrees in biology, plant pathology and science writing.

Volcano Erupts after Lying Dormant for 12,000 Years, Sending Scientists Scrambling

By Stephanie Pappas

A long-quiet volcano in Ethiopia spewed ash nine miles into the sky on Sunday, marking the first known major eruption from this volcano for more than 12,000 years.

Under-studied and situated in Ethiopia's arid, rural northeast, volcano Hayli Gubbi's towering ash column may be a clue to other, undetected eruptions in that period, says Juliet Biggs, an earth scientist at the University of Bristol in England.

"I would be really surprised if [more than 12,000 years ago] really is the last eruption date," Biggs says. While there have been no confirmed eruptions in that time span, satellite images hint that the volcano may have recently burped out lava, she says.

Either way, this eruption is highly unusual. Hayli Gubbi is a shield volcano, like Hawaii's Mauna Loa. These volcanoes are known for oozing lava flows, not expelling giant columns of ash.

"To see a big eruption column, like a big umbrella cloud, is really rare in this area," Biggs says.

Hayli Gubbi sits in the East African Rift Zone, a region where the African and Arabian plates are pulling apart at a rate of about 0.4 to 0.6 inches a year, says Arianna Soldati, a volcanologist at North Carolina State University. If the two plates keep moving apart, then eventually the Arabian Sea and rift valley will become a new ocean.

As the Earth's crust pulls apart, it stretches and thins, and hot rocks rise up from the mantle, melting into magma toward the surface.

"So long as there are still the conditions for magma to form, a volcano can still have an eruption even if it hasn't had one in 1,000 years, 10,000 years," Soldati says.

Researchers had some idea an eruption at Hayli Gubbi was possible, Biggs says. In July another active volcano nearby called Erta Ale erupted in a shower of ash. At the same time, satellite data revealed ground movement showing that an intrusion of magma from Erta Ale had pushed more than 18 miles below the surface, under Hayli Gubbi and beyond. Biggs and her collaborators had also recorded white puffy clouds at its summit, and the ground at the volcano had risen a few centimeters.

Sunday's eruption, which poses little danger to people given its remote location, has kicked off a scientific scramble. Derek Keir, an earth scientist at the University of Southampton in England, happened to be in Ethiopia when the volcano blew; on Monday he collected samples of the new ash. These will help reveal what kind of magma caused the eruption, Biggs says. Lava flows from the volcano could also reveal if Hayli Gubbi truly was quiet for 12,000 years.

"It really just shows how understudied this region is," Biggs says.

About the Author

Stephanie Pappas is a freelance science journalist based in Denver, Colo.

Giant Volcano Rewrites the Story of Seafloor Formation

By William W. Sager

Big, dark ocean waves were rolling our research ship from side to side. The *Falkor* is 83 meters long and weighs more than 2,000 metric tons, but a storm from Siberia that had just missed us was still churning the seas. Sitting in the science lab on the main deck, I was trying to keep my coffee from spilling onto my map of the seafloor.

It was mid-October 2015, and we were in the northwestern Pacific Ocean, about 1,600 kilometers east of Japan. For the umpteenth time I was looking at a map that showed somewhat parallel stripes along the seafloor around Tamu Massif, an enormous, ancient volcano. Each stripe indicated how a band of seafloor was magnetized–positively or negatively–but the pattern did not agree with how I thought Tamu Massif had erupted.

A sudden wave hit the *Falkor* with a loud thud, jarring me, and just then I realized what I had been missing. I had been studying this volcano for more than two decades. I had published the definitive papers giving the volcano its name and explaining its history. So my insight was only partly a "Eureka!" moment; the other part was a Homer Simpson moment: "D'oh!" My old ideas, and everyone else's, about how this volcano formed had been wrong.

Tamu Massif is special. It is roughly 430 kilometers wide and 600 kilometers long, covering an area similar to that of New Mexico. It is more than 50 times bigger than Mauna Loa on the island of Hawaii by volume, yet it is essentially flat. Its broad slopes dip by about one degree from the middle toward the edges, whereas a typical undersea volcano has a decline of five to 10 degrees. Imagine an entire football field covered by a taut gray tarp, with a stick just 60 centimeters high propping it up at midfield.

The volcano is the main mountain in one of the largest oceanic plateaus on the planet: Shatsky Rise. Yet the peak is still about 1,980 meters below the sea's surface. Most oceanic plateaus are made of basalt, implying that great volumes of magma rose from Earth's mantle and moved through the crust, squeezing up through the seafloor and pouring outward. Although Tamu Massif's shape seems to reflect this eruption process, the data I have collected since 2015 show that this is not what happened.

This new insight means scientists have misunderstood how dozens of immense underwater volcanoes have created more than 5 percent of the planet's current seafloor. Indeed, we have stumbled on an entirely new type of volcano.

If Tamu Massif or one of its cousins erupted again, it could make the Pacific Ocean more acidic, killing all kinds of marine life. It could also release large amounts of greenhouse gases into the ocean and the atmosphere. When we look back through history, it appears that eruptions from a similar volcano, the Ontong Java Plateau in the southwestern Pacific Ocean, corresponded with widespread, low-oxygen ocean conditions. Finally, although I am inspired by the thought that we are rewriting our ideas about the seafloor's formation, I also have to accept a hard reality: Tamu Massif, which had been branded "Earth's largest shield volcano," no longer deserves that title.

Piece of Cake

Tamu Massif formed gradually, over several million years, about 145 million years ago. During that period Earth's magnetic field reversed a couple of times at irregular intervals, leaving telltale magnetic stripes in the oceanic crust.

My first paper about Tamu Massif's magnetic history was published in 1993, when I was at Texas A&M University–the origin of "Tamu" (and massif means "massive" in French). In it, I concluded that the volcano must have formed from one eruption event in a short time: a huge blob of magma hundreds of kilometers in diameter rose through the mantle and spread out onto the seafloor. Massive eruptions caused floods of hot basalt to run down the accumulating slopes, building a broad, slightly domed layer of new earth. Subsequent eruptions would have added more layers, creating something like a layer cake, with the oldest basalt layer on the bottom and the youngest basalt layer at the top. On land, this is generally how shield volcanoes form. Other experts had similar thoughts about the world's largest oceanic plateaus: Ontong Java and the Kerguelen Plateau in the southern Indian Ocean.

After more research expeditions to further map Tamu Massif and take samples of its basalts, in 2013 my colleagues and I published a paper in Nature Geoscience indicating that Tamu Massif was an enormous shield volcano. Soon enough the media declared that we scientists had discovered "the world's largest shield volcano."

That superlative always made me cringe. I tried to tell journalists that we did not discover Tamu Massif (that happened in the early 20th century) and that there are larger oceanic plateaus. But something else bothered me: the pattern of magnetic stripes was odd for a broad shield that had formed like a layer cake.

If you looked down from space at the floor of the Pacific Ocean with glasses that revealed magnetism, you would see parallel stripes everywhere. But at a volcano, you would expect to see a big splatter mark because lava pouring out from the center would have interrupted that pattern. Not having such glasses, I had been collecting magnetic-field data at sea. My "Eureka!" moment on the *Falkor* happened when it became clear that there was indeed a wide, continuous stripe across Tamu Massif.

Tamu Massif formed at a triple junction—a place where three tectonic plates meet, like three huge wedges converging at a single point. When two of the plates spread apart, a crack opened along their boundary. Magma oozed up to fill the void and solidified as basalt. As the plates moved farther from the center, the new ribbon was torn along its axis and pulled apart, and newer magma filled the newer void.

This process repeated over and over. Tamu Massif was not built like a layer cake at all. Instead imagine a sheet cake being pulled apart horizontally, with new cake filling the crack that formed down the middle. That cake was subsequently pulled apart, newer cake filled the newer crack, and so on. If new ribbons of cake alternated between chocolate and vanilla, over time a pattern of stripes would be created. On Tamu Massif, positive and negative magnetic stripes correspond to this pattern.

There are two physical problems with this explanation, however. The stripes on Tamu Massif's southeastern quadrant turn 90 degrees counterclockwise. In retrospect, the reason for this seems somewhat obvious. As Tamu Massif erupted over time, a piece of the plate to the northeast broke off and moved, causing a segment near the triple junction to rotate 90 degrees. This segment is where Tamu Massif formed. Realizing that the stripe down Tamu Massif's back was a spreading magnetic anomaly was my "D'oh!" moment.

The second problem is that in the sheet-cake model, each newly formed ribbon of cake should have the same height as the existing cake being pulled apart. But Tamu Massif is thickest in the middle. I think this structure developed because the melting at the center increased for some time, forming a higher crust.

Tamu, Take Two

My colleagues and I have collected a lot of seafloor data and core samples drilled from area basalts that are helping us convince other scientists that our interpretation is correct. Our new understanding of Tamu Massif revolutionizes the view of how oceanic plateaus formed. Observations from a few other oceanic plateaus–those for which we have enough magnetic data to map the stripes–imply that many formed in a similar manner. Plateaus that developed where plates were diverging must be a new class of volcano. This means that the widely accepted assumption that oceanic plateaus are large shield volcanoes created by long basaltic lava flows is incorrect.

Why did we get the picture wrong before? And does it matter that Tamu Massif is not a classic shield volcano? We were wrong because submarine volcanoes hide under thousands of meters of water, so we cobbled together a picture from fragmental data. Imagine trying to reconstruct a dinosaur from just a tooth and a toe bone. You would attempt to connect them in a diagram based on what you know about other dinosaurs, but if your assumptions are incorrect, the picture will be incorrect, too. Tamu Massif is no longer the largest shield volcano on Earth, because it is not a shield volcano. We assumed that it formed like other volcanoes, but that was a bad assumption. Instead we found a new family of volcanic mountains–a new explanation for how giant features on Earth were formed. And there are dozens of them under the sea.

Scientists are always trying to understand how things came to be. That is our goal–even if it overrules our own prior findings. Our fresh understanding of Tamu Massif allows me to say, "We finally figured it out." That may not be as headline-worthy as "world's biggest," but I am happier with it.

About the Author

William W. Sager is a professor of geophysics at the University of Houston. He has sailed on 46 oceanographic expeditions and gave the Tamu Massif volcano its name.

Meet the Magnificent Microbes of the Deep Unknown

By Jeffery DelViscio

Jeffery DelViscio: You're listening to Science, Quickly. I'm Jeff DelViscio.

Now, we're not sure about all of you, but for us here on the show, some days we just want to explore. The unknown still exists all around us. And we have the super sweet day job of talking to folks who plumb the depths of those mysterious places. Today I'm joined by two explorers, and they literally seek out the deepest unknowns there are on this earth.

Karen Lloyd is a microbiologist at the University of Tennessee, though she's soon to be at the University of Southern California. And Peter Barry is a geochemist and volcanologist at the Woods Hole Oceanographic Institution. Hi, Karen. Hi, Peter.

Karen Lloyd: Hey.

Peter Barry: Hey, Jeff.

DelViscio: So thank you for joining us today. So maybe let's start off with this. Tell us about unknown places that you love the most and you seek out.

Peter, why don't you go first?

Barry: Sure, yeah. So, I am a vulcanologist and geochemist and I love to work in volcanic systems and hot springs all around the world. And what we try to do is visit different places where there's natural volcanic emissions. So there's there's gas, there's fluid coming to the surface. And what I do is I can collect those gases and those fluids and I can bring them back to my laboratory here in Massachusetts, and we can measure the chemistry of those systems.

I specialize in measuring stable isotopes, things like carbon and helium and other stable isotopes. And we can basically fingerprint these different volcanic systems to understand where the fluids and the gases in the material are coming from within Earth's deep interior. And I love traveling to subduction zones all over the world. And it's amazing that we see totally different signatures depending on where we go.

DelViscio: Very cool. Karen, what about you?

Lloyd: I was just thinking that it's really ironic that the place that we just got back from a couple of weeks ago was very high altitude. You think you want to go deep inside the earth, which is the thing we want to do, because that's where the unknown is. There's so little that we know about what's inside Earth's crust.

It's just hard to dig down to. You can't see through Earth. You can't drop something off the back of a ship and like we can in the oceans, you know, you have to drill and that's expensive and it takes years of preparation. So one thing that that Peter and I have been doing and our colleagues is using natural hot springs that sort of take some of that deep subsurface environment and shoot it all back up to the surface.

And we try to take these fluids as they come directly out of the ground. So where we were most recently was in the Puna region in Jujuy in Argentina with our colleague Agostina Chiodi. And so she's fantastic. She just like planned out this entire trip. It was such a heavy lift, but we drove all around. I think we drove over 8,000 kilometers in ten days or something like that.

Just sampling hot springs everywhere, dealing with splitting headaches and the nausea that comes from living above 15,000 feet every single day for ten days in a row with no lead in, no acclimatization. But we got some great, great samples. But I love that irony of to go deep, we have to go high.

DelViscio: You know, you're talking about two things that seem sort of not to be related if if you're not kind of looking closely. One is sort of deep rock stuff and then the other is, you know, microscopic life stuff. So like, how did you guys sort of get together scientifically speaking? Like, why are you working together if it seems like your disciplines are so different?

Lloyd: Can I guess now you want to do it.

Barry: You can do it. Karen, go ahead.

Lloyd: I had been thinking for years like, I need to figure out what's happening with microbes in the crust. And what I need is a geologist who actually wants to work with me and talk to me and is not like, oh, well, that's an interesting project, good luck, but actually will stick with me and help me. And I went to this meeting in 2015 and I had never met Peter before and he just pitched to the room this idea of combining deep subsurface microbiology with geology.

And I was like, I made a beeline. I ran over them. When as soon as he stopped talking, I was like, I want to do this.

Barry: Yeah, I was. I remember this conference and it dawned on me as I looked around the room that it's really kind of critical to not only have a geological perspective like I have, but also understand what's happening from a biological perspective and try to try to link those up.

DelViscio: Is there life down in the crust? It seems inhospitable in a lot of different ways, but is that true?

Lloyd: It only seems inhospitable if you have a narrow view of how life can exist on this earth. If you expand your understanding of the temperatures that life can handle or are the types of elements that life can breathe, then suddenly a lot more habitable space on this planet opens up to you. Right now, our estimates are that there are about 10,000 times more living cells in Earth's crust than there are number of stars in the universe.

So this is now a really significant biome on earth, and it's largely unknown. We're still asking really basic questions about it. So it's really fun to be asking fundamental questions in an environment that's so important for Earth, but we just don't know about it.

DelViscio: How does it compare to life on the surface, like biomass? Is there a way more down there than there is up here?

Lloyd: So the way to put it in the context of the total biomass on earth is that these are small cells, so they're much smaller biomass than what we have at the surface because just think about where the energy sources are coming from. At the surface, we've got this like gigantic blazing sun that basically powers trees and grass and stuff.

So we definitely have more total living biomass on the surface than we have in the subsurface. I want to be be clear about that. But the stuff that's in the subsurface is not just sad little crusts of life clinging to what falls down, that they can eat the leftovers of the dead animals and stuff there. Is that too. But there's additional sources of energy that are inside our earth that are supporting a separate ecosystem.

DelViscio: It's a heck of a lot of stuff we didn't know was there living stuff? How do you think about life as it exists in the crust?

Lloyd: We tend to think of life is being oriented around sunlight and seasons and day night cycles because we are addicted to the sun. We need all that energy to support our big hot bodies. But there's separate ecosystem in our Earth's crust is supported instead by energy coming from chemical reactions in Earth's crust. The two really big things are that they are independent of the timescales that we have up at the surface, which creates for some crazy long lived things.

And the other thing is that they are very diverse in what they can breathe. So we breathe oxygen. That's it. Every animal breathes oxygen when plants breathe, you know, during the day they make oxygen, but they also breathe at night. So they breathe oxygen. So up here, we're all like a one trick pony. And in the subsurface, suddenly transition metals in the middle of the periodic table, like become active for them.

They can use all this stuff. There are microbes that can breathe palladium and copper and nickel and antimony and vanadium and selenium and all these things. And arsenic. You know, that's something that's very toxic to us. But for them it's like oxygen. There's even an organism that can breathe carbon dioxide, like breathe. It is in, you know, reduce it in their cells to get energy.

Whereas for us, it's an end product. It's literally our waste. We can't do anything with CO2.

DelViscio: Ah, carbon dioxide. So Peter, as the geochemist here, how do you think about what you study and the carbon at the surface and what could be done with it at depth?

Barry: I try to understand what's happening from like a geological carbon cycle, how much carbon is coming out of volcanoes, how much is going back into the Earth's interior due to subduction processes and plate tectonic processes. And then that gives you a baseline for understanding what's happening with human emissions. We're not necessarily studying how these microbes could be used to sequester the carbon we have.

We're just we're just making that first order and link between, you know, the natural geological carbon cycle and where that carbon resides, where it could be trapped in Earth's crust, both due to geological processes and due to biological processes. Only in the last five, ten years have people really been focused on, you know, how could you potentially pull some of that carbon out, How could you sequester, how could you put it in these depleted oil and gas reservoirs and store for long geological periods?

So you're basically flipping, flipping it around, you know, instead of how quickly can you extract and burn it, how quickly could you sequester it and put it back in to sort of balance the system?

Lloyd: Well, one important thing to know is that there are natural deposits of CO2. You know, if we put down stuff in the form of carbon dioxide, there's precedent for that. So this is not so completely unnatural. You can see it is like a giant machine with lots of knobs and turning points. And a lot of those have big question marks on them right now.

You know, what does it take to tune the system to do what we want? How do we engineer things in the deep subsurface and that that it's going to take a lot more work like what we're doing, what other people are doing to see what's down there right now and what kinds of things they do.

DelViscio: I wanted to leave our listeners with a little bit of wonder if you had one thing you could tell them about the world we don't know under our feet. What would it be?

Barry: You know, we've really only understood plate tectonics for the last 50 or so years, and we have carbon and water and other volatiles moving between the Earth's surface and interior in this very dynamic system. You know, Earth is incredibly unique. And then seeing how that is actually influencing this, this really rich biology and microbiology that people like Karen study is absolutely fascinating to me because I have no doubt that the two are ultimately connected and that's what makes this planet so unique.

Lloyd: I think almost all of them are on deep branches of life that we don't know anything about. So we're talking about things that are is different from us as like a a sponge or even more different from us than a sponge, like something like a slime mold versus us. And there's like a hundreds of them. So that means that there's all these lineages that have been evolving to do something interesting or wonderful or strange or different, and we literally don't know what they're doing.

We have no idea what they're doing. So it's almost like having aliens here on Earth with us. They're not aliens. They're related to us. They're from Earth, but we just don't know anything about them. There is unknown to us is an alien would be.

DelViscio: That's great. And to all of you listeners, the yearning for more microbe. Karen and Peter have been rendered as adorable cartoon scientists and a film that we have on the site right now called Unearthed the borrowing to it and the transcript notes

FBI. It features a Scotch laden subsurface microbe named Mick and it's well worth the 5 minutes of your time.

Barry: For example, our buddy Mick, he's from about a mile below the Mariana Trench.

Mic the Microbe: People hear that I live under the Earth's crust and they're like, so you're from hell? But you know what? I'm just a regular dude. Mick, the microbe. Mickey I just happen to live inside the earth. And we get a different way of doing things down there.

DelViscio: Thanks for chatting with us today, Karen and Peter. Really appreciate it.

Lloyd: Thanks for having us.

Barry: Thanks a lot, Jeff.

DelViscio: Science, Quickly is produced by me, Jeff DelViscio, Kelso Harper and Tulika Bose. Our theme music was composed by Dominic Smith. Like and subscribe to Science, Quickly wherever you get your podcasts. And for more science news and long reads, head to sciam.com. For Science,Quickly, this is Jeff DelViscio.

About the Author

Jeffery DelViscio is currently chief multimedia editor/executive producer at Scientific American. He is former director of multimedia at STAT, where he oversaw all visual, audio and interactive journalism. Before that he spent more than eight years at the New York Times, where he worked on five different desks across the paper. He holds dual master's degrees in journalism and in Earth and environmental sciences from Columbia University. He has worked onboard oceanographic research vessels and tracked money and politics in science from Washington, D.C. He was a Knight Science Journalism Fellow at the Massachusetts Institute of Technology in 2018. His work has won numerous awards, including two News and Documentary Emmy Awards.

Mangrove Trees Are on the Move, Taking the Tropics with Them

By Michael Adno

Two decades ago ecologist Ilka C. Feller heard about a plant advancing at an unprecedented rate into a coastal restoration site near Merritt Island on Florida's Atlantic coast, midway between Miami and Georgia's southern border. The plant was a mangrove, a tree that thrives in salt water and grows in stands along the ocean's edge. The tree's roots form a tangle that extends several feet out of the water, and its thin, tawny trunk and branches reach up into a dense canopy of waxy, jadelike leaves. Stands can stretch for miles, forming a biologically diverse forest that builds land by trapping sediment and protects coastlines from erosion, waves and storm surges. Mangroves have long defended coasts against hurricanes, cyclones and tsunamis, which researchers have shown are more deadly along shores without the tangled trees. Mangroves capture vast amounts of carbon, too.

There are more than 70 species of mangrove, adapted to hot habitats with soil low in oxygen. They filter out almost all the salt that enters their roots and thrive in places where few other plants can. They grow around the world but only at tropical and subtropical latitudes, in places that don't have periodic freezes, which can prevent the plants from becoming established. Mangroves were not supposed to be at Merritt Island, but when Feller showed up in 2002 and started looking around, there they were.

Feller then drove to Tomoka State Park, about 70 miles farther north along the Atlantic coast. A park ranger told Feller there were no mangroves there, but she decided to look anyway. Sure enough, a few hundred yards past the ranger station she found small mangrove shrubs dotting the salt marsh. The following morning she drove another 40 miles north toward St. Augustine, Fla., which is only

60 miles south of the Georgia line, and she found a few isolated mangroves there, too.

Over the next 20 years Feller and her colleagues documented the poleward migration of mangroves in North America–and, by proxy, the shifting border of the subtropics. Since 1980 the world has lost more than 35 percent of its mangroves because of development, pollution and extreme weather. In parts of southern Florida, more than 50 percent have been destroyed. Yet in northern Florida, on the East Coast, mangroves have doubled in area. In Australia, the trees are migrating east to west rather than poleward. In Brazil, mangroves are creeping inland as rising seas push salt water deeper into the interior. And in South Africa, mangroves are migrating south, extending the subtropical boundary just as they are in Florida. It's unclear how far the mangroves will travel. But the migration offers a picture of the future as temperatures climb, weather patterns shift and sea levels rise. And recent discoveries have reshaped almost everything scientists thought about their movements.

Feller began her career in 1975 as a scientific illustrator at the Smithsonian Institution. Her interest in mangroves began after she met a sponge curator who learned she was an experienced scuba diver. The curator asked Feller to develop an underwater drawing technique. Feller agreed, and soon she was depicting the coral reef off Belize on sheets of drafting film fastened to a plexiglass drawing board. She later joined that curator to research mangroves in Panama, where she swam up channels through remote mangrove forests with her drawing system. She drew the roots and the juvenile fish swimming among them, as well as seagrass and corals. When she wasn't drawing, she collected insects. "I felt I could be there by myself all day and be totally happy," Feller says. "It just turned out to be a place that I fit."

Engrossed by the plants, Feller left Central America and went back to school for a Ph.D. in ecology. In 1997, just after turning 50, she returned to the Smithsonian as an ecologist. "I couldn't believe I got a job," she says. In the past two decades Feller, now 77, has established research sites throughout the

Caribbean, Belize, Panama, Ecuador, Australia and New Zealand, as well as Florida and the Gulf of Mexico's rim, studying the role of nutrients in mangrove stands, the species bound to the plants and the trees' migration. She is an author on more than 700 papers, including studies involving fieldwork in Saudi Arabia, Brazil and Indonesia, and she is widely regarded as a pioneer of experimental mangrove ecology. Some call Feller the godmother of mangrove ecology. Others call her "the mangrove queen." (Her friends call her Candy.)

In the early 2000s Feller started recording mangroves she found north of St. Augustine, in the space between two different types of habitat, an ecosystem transition known as an ecotone. This region is where she could find clues to how the coastline would change as freezes became less frequent and hurricanes became more frequent. Storm currents can carry mangrove seeds far away, helping to broaden their range. But storms can harm the trees, too; in 2019 high winds, storm surge and prolonged floods from Hurricane Dorian destroyed more than half the mangrove forests of Grand Bahama.

More mangrove habitat could be a promising defense against sea-level rise. The trees also sequester more carbon than any other plant, both above and below the ground, another counter to climate change. But they could also overtake salt marshes, with consequences. The marshes–vast, open areas of green, grassy wetlands bisected by serpentine creeks, flooded daily by tides–line parts of coasts in the U.S. and many other countries. They support vegetation, host imperiled bird species and filter water, helping coastal ecosystems flourish. About 75 percent of U.S. salt marshes are in the Southeast, precisely where mangroves are appearing. Although mangroves build land faster than salt marshes do–in some cases, four times as fast–they're much more vulnerable to cold temperatures. One severe freeze could eviscerate a forest, leaving the soft land vulnerable to erosion. "You could have that wetland go to water real quick," says William "Ches" Vervaeke, an ecologist with the National Park Service.

In Florida, there are three species of mangrove: red, black and white. The red mangroves grow closest to the water, the black a bit farther in from the water's edge, and the white in the higher elevations along the coast. Strangely, the three species are not related, but over millions of years they evolved in the same harsh environment. They resemble one another in form and location and in how they reproduce.

By the time summer rains begin in Florida, red mangroves put out delicate chartreuse flowers, which will eventually bear fruit. Then a long, pen-shaped propagule with a lithe curve appears. If you pry open a mature propagule with your fingernail, you will find a seedling ready to fall out. The propagules drop off the plant–often into the water, where they may be carried a few inches or hundreds of miles. White mangroves produce tinier flowers, densely organized fruit and a propagule the size of a green bean. The black mangrove's propagule is slightly larger and asymmetrical.

As spring turned to summer in 2016, Feller's search took her up Florida's east coast until she finally headed into Nassau County, the state's northeasternmost county, where the Nassau River meets the sea. One afternoon she and a postdoctoral researcher were driving on a long, low bridge over the river toward Amelia Island, just shy of the Georgia line, when an emerald shrub in the distance caught their eye. They hit the brakes, parked and ran under the bridge toward the marsh. On the other side of a tidal creek, a black mangrove stood like a sentry. At 30.3 degrees north, the specimen was situated one third of the way between the equator and the North Pole, 60 miles north of its previously recorded range–by far the northernmost mangrove in the U.S. Later, they called it "Candy's Mangrove."

Soon after, Feller's peers started to find other black mangroves in that same area. Then, in 2021, Vervaeke was running a skiff along the Fort George River a few miles south of Amelia Island. Breaks of cedar trees line the bluffs along the river where dense stands of oaks are littered with resurrection ferns and orchids. The place "is kind of a hidden gem," he says. That day Vervaeke looked out from the small boat and spotted a set of bright green leaves amid the dull spartina grass. He realized he'd found a red mangrove, the northernmost in America, a companion to Candy's black mangrove. "I almost literally jumped out of the boat to go and look at that thing," he says.

Vervaeke expected to find black mangroves because they can tolerate lower temperatures to some extent, but a red mangrove was unprecedented. The species defied logic, proliferating on various banks of various rivers. "The intriguing part that captures my imagination," says ecologist Scott F. Jones, an assistant professor at the University of North Florida, "is that we still don't understand and therefore can't predict where exactly mangroves are going to show up."

Early one morning last December, Vervaeke led me through a tiny clump of cedar trees and sabal palms and into a marsh just north of Jacksonville, Fla., where the Fort George River meets the Atlantic in a plateau of sand banks flanking spartina grass and narrow channels. About 100 yards ahead of us Jones and Feller were examining leaves of mangrove shrubs. They were looking for signs of a type of crab and an insect, called a psyllid, that are typically found on trees farther south. As the trees creep north, so should the species tied to them.

At one point, my head was buried inside a small shrub, following Feller's fingers as she aged the tree by counting sections of stem between nodes on its branches, which corresponded to seasons of growth (summer, long section; winter, short section.) Over time researchers noticed that active hurricane seasons were often followed by mild winters, which helped young plants take root after the storms spread propagules north.

Later that day Jones, Vervaeke, Feller and I headed north to the rim of Amelia Island to visit Candy's Mangrove. A light rain fell as we walked out toward the site. When we reached the ribbon of water separating the beach from the strand of marsh, it was too deep to cross without swimming. We opted for a warm lunch instead, waiting for the tide to drop. As we turned back toward the car, a bald eagle flew along a break of slash pines before landing in a nest. I wondered what the migration of this plant into the marsh would mean for birds and other animals, especially if mangroves replace salt marsh. The contrast between the two habitats is stark.

With more mangrove habitat, "there is a probable win for birds in many ways," Andrew Farnsworth, a visiting scientist at the Cornell University Lab of Ornithology, later told me. Mangroves in southern Florida are essential habitat for migratory species, and more than 30 percent of Europe's avian population spends winters in mangrove forests in West Africa. "Of course," Farnsworth said, "this will be at the cost of some salt marsh specialists" such as eastern black rails, whimbrels and salt marsh sparrows.

Any real-world transformation probably wouldn't be so simple. "I think these places are going to be a matrix of both salt marshes and mangroves," says Samantha Chapman, a biology professor at Villanova University. But in some areas, she says, it might be a "total transition." She thinks that, over time, there will be push and pull, creating additional habitat for some species while inevitably forcing others to look elsewhere. Many Florida game fish, for example, especially snook and tarpon, use mangrove estuaries as nurseries. In the past decade, however, researchers have found those juvenile snook and tarpon in marshes where there are no mangroves, including spots as far north as South Carolina. This shift shows that the fish can survive in varied habitats, and if other forces such as rising sea temperatures push them farther north, they may be able to adapt.

In other places, changes are more peculiar. Along the northern edge of the Amazon Delta, mangroves have been expanding inland as the rising sea inundates the low-lying coast. In some cases, that water follows navigational channels carved by residents and even the trails trod by wild water buffalo, forging paths along which salt water can creep inland and propagules can drift. The migration is "quite striking," says Carlos David Santos, an ecologist and assistant professor at the NOVA School of Science and Technology in Portugal, who has been monitoring 500 miles of uninterrupted mangrove forest in Brazil. Some formerly freshwater lakes there are now composed entirely of salt water, displacing fish such as arapaima that are favored by local communities. What disturbs Santos and others is how quickly changes are taking place: as habitat for shorebirds and macro invertebrates disappears along the coast, critical wetlands farther inland are rapidly becoming tight-knit mangrove forests.

Along the mouth of the Leichhardt River in Australia, increased precipitation and increased sediment accumulation have caused mangroves to expand out into the Gulf of Carpentaria; just a few miles west, mangroves are trending inland owing to prolonged periods of wetland flooding. In New Zealand, researchers have documented a rapid seaward migration of mangroves around Auckland. Over time people there altered rivers to suit agriculture, and increased sediment, coupled with higher levels of nitrogen and phosphorus from field runoff, has driven the mangroves' migration.

After tracking the movement of mangroves up Florida's coastline, Feller started to search through historical texts, looking for any clues about the trees' earlier whereabouts. That's when she found an anecdote that reshaped everything researchers knew about their range in the U.S.

In 1867 naturalist John Muir set out on foot for a journey across the South. His account of the trek was published posthumously in a 1916 book, *A Thousand-Mile Walk to the Gulf*. At one point, Muir crossed the St. Marys River from Georgia into Florida. As his boat drifted toward Fernandina Beach, a town on the river just south of the state line, he saw "clumps of mangrove and forests of moss-dressed, strange trees appearing low in the distance." This would have been roughly 15 miles north of Candy's Mangrove. If the description was accurate, the current consensus that mangroves had never grown so far north was wrong. Feller eventually found another mention from 1837 and a record from 1821. She ended up tracing the trail back to 1788, when French botanist and explorer André Michaux found mangroves south of Candy's.

Feller then sketched a time line of freezes based on citrus growers' records, along with a map of hurricane paths. (After

Hurricane Irma in 2017, Feller found mangrove propagules along the beach on Jekyll Island, 20 miles north of the Georgia line. She even found intact roots and branches.) She sent all these notes to Kyle Cavanaugh, an assistant professor at the University of California, Los Angeles, Institute of the Environment and Sustainability. Cavanaugh collected climate data for the Florida coast from 1950 to 2017. And Wilfrid Rodriguez, a researcher at the Smithsonian, pulled together aerial images of the Matanzas Inlet just south of St. Augustine going back to 1942. Together the records, data and imagery revealed a curious expansion and contraction of mangroves.

The team concluded, in a 2019 paper, that mangroves were not simply migrating north. Instead there was sophisticated, long-term movement of plants both northward and southward–"regime shifts" dictated by weather. Freezes pushed the mangrove boundary south. Often the habitat was replaced by salt marsh. But during mild winters and active hurricane seasons, mangrove forests slowly migrated north again.

In northeastern Florida, fluid transformations between mangroves and salt marsh occurred at least six times between the late 1700s and 2017, Feller says. But the researchers say that with annual temperatures rising relentlessly, freezes decreasing and hurricanes becoming more powerful, the northward migration of mangroves in recent years may become permanent. Soon enough, mangroves will spill into Georgia and then inevitably into South Carolina. The trees aren't simply marching north; they are taking leaps when the elements allow and falling back only slightly, if at all, when cool air reaches south.

In January 2024 Vervaeke and Jones invited me to join them as they looked for the next biological borderland of the subtropics. They dropped a skiff into the Nassau River, a few miles north of Candy's Mangrove, and headed north as the tide rose, carving through the backcountry until we reached the Intracoastal Waterway, which runs north to south. The first stretch of our search didn't yield anything. Four miles farther north, though, we all shouted, "There!" The unmistakable hue of a red mangrove sat beside a stand of cedar trees. Vervaeke and Jones were ecstatic; this was farther north than any other mangrove they had seen, and it was a red, too. Minutes later we found yet another red mangrove–the new northernmost tree. Using a GPS device, a computer tablet and an orange notebook, Vervaeke and Jones recorded the coordinates, elevation and plant measurements.

We continued north toward Fernandina Beach. Less than five minutes later, Jones pointed: "There." Another mangrove, this time a black one. The day continued like that as we found tree after tree farther and farther north–in the Amelia River, along Lanceford Creek and deep in the network of marshes that make up Tiger Island near Georgia's southern border. By the time we reached the state line, where the St. Marys River runs into the Atlantic, we had recorded 19 successive "northernmost" mangroves, most of which were red.

With the wind dropping, Vervaeke couldn't resist making an unplanned run across the river into Georgia. The marsh there feels endless, the live oaks along the shoreline ancient. The vast span of the St. Marys River pours out toward Cumberland Island, between the lime-green edges of the marsh. As we pressed against another shoreline, one plant poked up above the grass. Jones was skeptical, but Vervaeke smiled. Could it really be a mangrove, the first in Georgia? As Vervaeke set the boat onto an oyster bar, Jones ran over toward the plant. He reached the top of the bank and looked back, beaming. Vervaeke just laughed and gathered his equipment. "I'll be damned," he said.

On the run home, Vervaeke, who had tattooed the prior northernmost mangrove's coordinates on his arm, thought about making an appointment to update it. Back in the truck, they called Feller to tell her they'd found 21 new northernmost mangroves. Two of them were in Georgia. "No way!" the mangrove queen shouted. "I'll be there soon."

About the Author

Michael Adno lives in Sarasota, Fla., and has written for the New York Times, *the* New Yorker *and the* Bitter Southerner, *where he won a James Beard Award for his profile of folklorist Ernest Matthew Mickler.*

Section 5: How Climate Change is Impacting Untouched Places

5.1 How Climate Change Is Leaving Some Species with "Nowhere Left to Go"
By Fionna M. D. Samuel

5.2 The Reason Antarctica Is Melting: Shifting Winds, Driven by Global Warming
By Annie Sneed

5.3 Humans Have Crossed 7 of 9 'Planetary Boundaries'
By Andrea Thompson

How Climate Change Is Leaving Some Species with "Nowhere Left to Go"

By Fionna M. D. Samuels

For millennia, many animals and plants have coped with occasional climate changes by moving into new areas. But humans' relatively recent burning of fossil fuels is pushing global temperatures upward at an exceptionally rapid rate, placing many species on what a new book by science journalist Benjamin von Brackel notes has been called an "escalator to extinction"–and raising the question of whether migration can save them this time. It is estimated that land-dwelling animals are now moving toward the poles at a rate of an average of about 17 kilometers (more than 10 miles) per decade and that the front line of ocean dwellers is now doing so at a rate of 72 kilometers (45 miles) per decade. Some plant and animal species–such as the Edith's checkerspot butterfly and the Scots pine–are shifting to higher, cooler elevations in the mountains as well. What happens when they all run out of places to flee the heat?

His book *Nowhere Left to Go: How Climate Change Is Driving Species to the Ends of the Earth* (The Experiment Publishing) came out on July 5. In it, von Brackel examines this question and others that have arisen from the massive migrations spurred by global warming. The book discusses the research into how ecosystems might change as old species leave and new ones arrive, as well as the substantial implications for human societies.

Scientific American spoke with von Brackel about what science is telling us we can expect from having so many species on the move and how we might help some persist in the face of climate change.

[*An edited transcript of the interview follows*.]

Where did the idea for this book come from?

It was a couple of years ago, when I had been reading a study on ocean acidification, and there was this passing mention that cod are moving hundreds of kilometers north in the North Sea. I had to read the sentence twice. I thought, "Okay, wow, if the cod is doing this, maybe other fish species are doing this, too, and maybe other land-dwelling creatures also–and maybe all species on Earth." In my mind's eye I saw some kind of living tsunami rolling over the planet and confronting human societies. I thought, "Okay, wow, this could be huge." When I found out that this is actually happening–and except for the scientists dealing with this, nobody knows about the extent of this phenomenon–I thought, "Okay, well, I have to immerse myself in it."

What happens to species that can't move anymore?

The species that are not able to move and to conquer new places, they have a high risk of becoming extinct–that's it. Right now many species can move poleward. In latitudes like Europe or North America, species are expanding, so they can have new ranges. But the problem is in the tropics. There you have tropical mountains, where we now see the first species becoming extinct because they are at some point at the summit, so they can't move anywhere. It's a dead end.

The book talks about how insects and animals moving into new areas can bring health threats to humans. What are some of those potential threats?

I think it's one of the issues we should be most concerned about in terms of species range shifts. Let's take the Asian tiger mosquito [which can spread pathogens, including the dengue viruses and West Nile virus]. This insect is already conquering much of the U.S. and Europe. They initially came from Asia via international shipping to the U.S. in, I think, the 1980s–and then, afterward, to Italy in the 1990s. It was funny, because, two weeks ago, I was in Italy, and I wondered, "What are all these little mosquitoes biting me all the time?" Then I took a close look and I saw the zebralike white stripes on it. They actually were Asian tiger mosquitoes and, oh my God, I clobbered so many of them.

What are the possible economic impacts of these mass migrations?

There are already a lot. For example, in Germany, the two most important tree species for timber production are the Scots pine and European spruce, and their ranges are both retracting because of climate change. So they retract up the mountains, and they retract to Scandinavia. This has huge impacts, because models say that by the year 2100, 20 to 60 percent of the forest land will only be suitable for Mediterranean oak forest types—and they have much lower economic output.

Are there species that might leave a cultural loss as they move away?

Probably the people most affected by species shifts are Indigenous people, and that's because they live close to nature, and many of them depend on specific animals or plants. Many of them have circled their whole culture around just one species—like the Inupiat in Alaska, who hunt bowhead whales. Bowhead whales now migrate much farther north. That's a big problem for the Inupiat. Everything is changing, and they can't easily adapt by choosing another species as their main species.

Is there a similar situation with the disappearing kelp forests in Japan? That was another example you mention in the book that seems like a big shift, considering how central kelp and the fish species found in kelp forests are to Japanese culture and cuisine.

The kelp forests, on one hand, are so important for the Japanese as a food resource but also culturally. They do everything to protect them, but in the end, they can't stop this process. Maybe one good thing is that the species that follow the kelp forests are corals, so they have new coral reefs emerge. I find that kind of magical.

That was actually something that I took away as a glimmer of hope: some of the most at-risk species are moving, so maybe they won't go extinct.

I think this is the main message in the book: that species are able to respond to climate change. So this is a positive thing. In the last 2.6 million years of the ice age, there were many times that species had to respond to climate warming and climate cooling. And the interesting thing is that every time there were not many species that did go extinct. So they managed to do this. And this is a very hopeful thing.

What is different about today?

The thing that's different today is us. First of all, we have occupied so many places on Earth–about half the surface of Earth–with agricultural land and cities. And we also crisscrossed the land with streets and canals. That makes it very hard for many species to move to respond to climate change.

How can we help species adapt to this very drastic change in climate?

So the most important and most obvious thing is to curb emissions. Without stopping climate change and curbing emissions fast enough, species don't have a chance. But on the way to do this, we can do a lot of other things. In general, we have to give species the room to respond to climate change and to create enough conservation areas where they can thrive and to connect them with enough wildlife corridors–and that's starting to happen already. Some scientists recommend protecting about 30 percent of Earth's surface and some even more–around 50 percent. In fact, at the United Nations Biodiversity Conference, coming up in autumn, nations are about to decide on [how much land to protect]. So this is a real possibility, and I think this will be an important first step. But afterward, one has to see, "Okay, where are the conservation areas built?" and "Will this be implemented?"

Can individual people help by, for example, not growing lawns?

I think everybody who has a garden can help species to create a stepping-stone so that they can move to higher latitudes. And yeah, as you said, a lawn isn't very helpful. Here in Berlin, I see many gardens that are even paved or full of gravel–and that's also not very helpful. What you can do is to have a hedge instead of a fence, to have fruit trees and berry bushes where bumblebees or honeybees can thrive or have little branch piles so birds and rodents can hide. You can do a lot with the garden.

About the Author

Fionna M. D. Samuels was a 2022 AAAS Mass Media Fellow at Scientific American. *She's pursuing a Ph.D. in chemistry at Colorado State University. Follow her on Twitter @Fairy__Hedgehog*

The Reason Antarctica Is Melting: Shifting Winds, Driven by Global Warming

By Annie Sneed

In the remote, alien area of the world where the Amundsen Sea meets the coast of West Antarctica, tall, frozen cliffs loom over the water. They are the edges of massive glaciers–rivers of ice that spill into the ocean. In recent years, these icy rivers have been flowing and melting at an alarming rate, threatening to add a substantial amount of water to the sea that would eat away at global coastlines.

For a long time, scientists had suspected that man-made climate change was likely causing this area of West Antarctica's ice to thin, but they had not established a direct connection or mechanism. The issue is critical because this is where the majority of the continent's ice loss is occurring. Now a new study published this week in *Nature Geoscience* appears to have solved the puzzle. A team of researchers in the U.S. and the U.K. found that global warming has caused a shift in wind patterns that are ultimately bringing more warm ocean water into contact with the region's ice.

Climate scientists first began to notice that all was not right with West Antarctica's ice a couple of decades ago, but its melt proved a bit enigmatic. For the most part, air temperatures are still too cold for surface melting to explain why the ice is thinning. That fact suggested the ocean was likely the culprit–yet the top layer of seawater is also too cold to thaw the ice. And while there is a deeper layer of warm ocean water that sometimes reaches the Amundsen Sea and laps away at the undersides of two giant glaciers in the region–called Pine Island and Thwaites–rising global temperatures were not directly warming that water.

"This is an area where the [warm] ocean waters that melt the ice have been out of contact with the atmosphere for thousands of years," explains Paul Holland, an ice-ocean scientist at the British Antarctic Survey and one of the authors of the new study. "They're very old waters, so they wouldn't have been [heated] by global warming." Thus, the question for Holland and his team was if–and how–climate change had affected these deep-ocean waters. They suspected that wind might be the missing connection.

Holland and his colleagues combined wind data, satellite observations of sea-ice drift and climate-model simulations to understand how wind patterns near Antarctica have evolved since the 1920s (which is how far back the simulations extend) and how any changes may have affected glaciers that flow into the Amundsen Sea. They compared different simulations to parse which effects came from natural fluctuations in the climate versus anthropogenic climate change.

They found that wind patterns indeed appear to have changed over the past century–and in a way that can explain the increased melting of the West Antarctic ice sheet. In the 1920s, the team reports, the winds over the Amundsen Sea would have predominantly blown toward the west, mostly keeping the warm ocean water at bay. But today the wind patterns flip-flop between blowing eastward and westward. When the waters blow toward the east, the deep layer of warm ocean water can creep in. "When the wind blows east, you get these rivers of warm water coming into the [Amundsen Sea] and melting the ice," Holland explains. "It's basically like turning on a hot tap when the wind blows toward the east and turning off the tap when the wind blows toward the west."

The reason climate change is causing this shift is because of the fundamental way wind works on the earth and responds to warming, Holland says. The earth's surface is warming unevenly, which influences where areas of high and low pressure are situated in the atmosphere overhead. Because winds flow between those highs and lows, warming affects the broad patterns of winds across the globe. In West Antarctica, warming is shifting a key band of winds southward and making it stronger, which ultimately causes the winds over the Amundsen Sea to blow east.

Other scientists say that this study provides critical insights into what is going on in Antarctica and what could continue tohappen as the planet warms. While many questions remain, "this study increases our scientific confidence that the retreat of West Antarctic ice contributing to sea-level rise was triggered by human-caused global warming," says Richard Alley, ageoscientist at Pennsylvania State University, who also studies Antarctica but was not involved in this work.

Ted Scambos, a senior research scientist at the University of Colorado Boulder, who was also not involved with the new study, agrees. "We had been able to detect that Pine Island and Thwaites [glaciers] were thinning rapidly and flowing faster," he says. "Something had changed, and they're maybe starting down the road of taking all the ice off West Antarctica. How did that happen?" The study's findings are "a good framework for the climate events that lead to ice loss from this area of West Antarctica," he adds.

The region's future is, to some degree, in our hands. The study authors also looked at how Antarctica's wind patterns would respond if humans are able to reduce the production of greenhouse gases–or if they do not do so. "If we carry on emitting greenhouse gases at an uncontrolled rate, then by 2100, we'll have winds that reliably blow toward the east"–meaning the winds that bring in the layer of deep warm water, Holland explains. But if humans rein in their emissions so that they start falling by 2050 and ultimately stabilize at half of the current rate, wind patterns could be kept in their current state. "It will require some serious and urgent effort on the part of humankind," Holland says, "but is less ambitious than the target of the Paris climate agreement."

That stabilized point may still not be an ideal situation, because West Antarctic ice is already melting at a faster rate than it would have without a human-altered climate–yet it is better than nothing. "If we are able to restrict the amount of further warming, then the effects of this change in the future will be less extreme," says Scambos, who is co-leading a major study of Thwaites Glacier. "We probably can't stop everything, but we can put the brakes on if we begin to act."

About the Author

Annie Sneed is a science journalist who has written for the New York Times, Wired, *Public Radio International and* Fast Company.

Humans Have Crossed 7 of 9 "Planetary Boundaries"

By Andrea Thompson

Our planet is sick, and its life-threatening symptoms are getting worse, a new report warns.

Earth has been pushed past multiple physical and chemical boundaries crucial for keeping the world a livable place. Beyond already exceeded thresholds set by scientists for rising temperatures, biodiversity loss and chemical pollution, we have now also breached the boundary on ocean acidification. The milestone comes with grim ramifications for marine ecosystems and human livelihoods.

"More than three-quarters of the Earth's support systems are not in the safe zone," Johan Rockström, director of the Potsdam Institute for Climate Impact Research (PIK) in Germany, said in a statement announcing the 2025 evaluation of the planetary boundaries. "Humanity is pushing beyond the limits of a safe operating space, increasing the risk of destabilizing the planet."

Humans and many other species evolved to thrive in the climate of the Holocene, a period that began around 10,000 years ago. But as societies industrialized and began widely burning fossil fuels in the 19th century, greenhouse gases built up in the atmosphere, trapping heat and transforming Earth and its climate in many ways besides raising global temperatures.

Beginning in 2009, PIK flagged and prioritized research on nine geophysical limits that make up a sort of planetary life-support system; staying within these limits, they argue, is the best hope for maintaining the clement climatic conditions we and most of Earth's other denizens have adapted to. In 2023 researchers published a study that quantified those boundaries and established where we are in relation to them. At the time, six of the boundaries had been surpassed, with many well into what the scientists called a "zone of increasing risk."

"It's like blood pressure," said the 2023 study's lead author Katherine Richardson, an earth systems scientist at the University of Copenhagen, in an interview with Scientific American at the time. "If your blood pressure is over 120 over 80, it's not a guarantee that you're going to have a heart attack, but it does raise the risk, and therefore we do what we can to bring it down."

Among the nine boundaries is of course climate change, which is measured in part by the amount of world-warming carbon dioxide in Earth's atmosphere. Carbon dioxide concentrations reached a record global high of 422.7 parts per million (ppm) last year, compared with 280 ppm prior to the industrial revolution and the 350 ppm that many scientists consider a "safe" limit (which was surpassed in 1987). The burning of fossil fuels is the indisputable culprit.

Fossil fuels are also behind the new boundary breaching–the ocean absorbs some of the atmosphere's excess carbon dioxide, causing waters to become more acidic. Since the industrial revolution, the ocean's surface pH has dropped by 0.1; this may seem minuscule, but because the pH scale is logarithmic, it reflects roughly a 30 percent increase in acidity.

Ocean acidification can have profound impacts on marine ecosystems by depleting seawater of certain carbon compounds that corals and other shell building animals need to construct their protective homes. At low enough pH levels, corals and shells can even begin to dissolve. These effects could destabilize entire ecosystems and devastate many commercially valuable species, such as oysters. A 2020 report by the U.S. National Oceanic and Atmospheric Administration found that ocean acidification would cost the country's economy billions of dollars.

"The movement we're seeing is absolutely headed in the wrong direction. The ocean is becoming more acidic, oxygen levels are dropping, and marine heatwaves are increasing. This is ramping up pressure on a system vital to stabilize conditions on planet Earth," Levke Caesar, co-lead of PIK's Planetary Boundaries Science Lab, said in the new evaluation's press statement.

The not-so-short list of other boundaries we've blown past is sobering. Excess phosphorus and nitrogen from the widespread use of fertilizers flows into rivers and seas to spark toxic algal blooms. Artificial chemicals, such as plastics, dichlorodiphenyltrichloroethane (DDT) and "forever chemical" perfluoroalkyl and polyfluoroalkyl substances (PFAS) disruptively accumulate in food chains. Agriculture and other changes in land use strip away forests and diminish available fresh water. And as all these problems grow, more and more of Earth's biodiversity is disappearing.

According to the new report, just two of the nine limits remain intact: ozone depletion and aerosols in the atmosphere. Only the former shows clear progress away from the planetary boundary, as a result of the success of the Montreal Protocol, the international agreement through which countries are phasing out chemicals that erode Earth's protective ozone layer. Aerosol emissions have declined globally–partly from efforts to reduce pollution from global shipping–but absent any unified policy framework for reductions, levels could easily surge back.

The overall prognosis for the planet's health is poor, given that a number of countries, including the U.S. in particular, are moving away from meaningful action to tackle environmental problems.

"We are witnessing widespread decline in the health of our planet. But this is not an inevitable outcome. The drop in aerosol pollution and healing of the ozone layer, shows that it is possible to turn the direction of global development. Even if the diagnosis is dire, the window of cure is still open," Rockström said in the press statement. "Failure is not inevitable; failure is a choice. A choice that must and can be avoided."

About the Author

Andrea Thompson is senior desk editor for life science at Scientific American, *covering the environment, energy and earth sciences. She has been covering these issues for nearly two decades. Prior to joining* Scientific American, *she was a senior writer covering climate science at* Climate Central *and a reporter and editor at* Live Science, *where she primarily covered earth science and the environment. She has moderated panels, including as part of the United Nations Sustainable Development Media Zone, and appeared in radio and television interviews on major networks. She holds a graduate degree in science, health and environmental reporting from New York University, as well as a B.S. and an M.S. in atmospheric chemistry from the Georgia Institute of Technology. Follow Thompson on Bluesky @andreatweather.bsky.social*

GLOSSARY

altimeter A device that measures the height of an object.

autonomous Having freedom to act independently.

biodiversity The variety of all living things on the earth.

bioluminescence Light emitted from a living thing through a chemical reaction.

biomolecule Small particles made by living things, which are the basis for life.

chemosynthetic Creating energy and food by using a chemical reaction of sunlight.

dark oxygen Oxygen made on the deep sea floor without using photosynthesis or sunlight.

enigma Something that is difficult to understand.

enzyme A special type of protein that speeds up chemical reactions without being used up in the process.

fissures A long narrow crack in a surface.

hydrothermal The action of hot water that's been heated underground, circulating and creating new minerals.

invertebrate An animal that doesn't have a bony skeleton.

menagerie A collection of unusual animals, especially for an exhibition.

microbe A small organism that is too small to be seen by the naked eye.

osmolyte A molecule that maintains hydration, stabilizes proteins, and protects the organism from drought and high temperature.

oxidation A chemical process in which something loses electrons by either adding oxygen or removing hydrogen.

perpetuity Something that continues without an end date.

porous Something that has a lot of holes or gaps that allow liquids to pass through.

substrate The base on which another chemical reaction or material exists.

terrestrial Something that is land-dwelling.

FURTHER INFORMATION

Copley, Jon, and The Conversation UK. "Just How Little Do We Know About the Ocean Floor?" *Scientific American*. October 9, 2014. www.scientificamerican.com/article/just-how-little-do-we-know-about-the-ocean-floor/.

Fieseler, Clare, and Jason Jaacks. "A 'Dark Oxygen' Mystery Is Unfolding at the Ocean Bottom—But Undersea Mining Giants May Soon Move In." *Scientific American*. July 24, 2025. www.scientificamerican.com/video/polymetallic-nodules-a-source-of-rare-metals-may-hold-the-secrets-of-dark/.

Harvey, Chelsea, and E&E News. "Thousands of New Creatures Discovered in Deep-Sea Mining Zone." *Scientific American*. May 26, 2023. www.scientificamerican.com/article/thousands-of-new-creatures-discovered-in-deep-sea-mining-zone/.

Harvey, Chelsea, and E&E News. "Warming May Push Ecosystems to Release Carbon Instead of Absorbing It." *Scientific American*. January 14, 2021. www.scientificamerican.com/article/warming-may-push-ecosystems-to-release-carbon-instead-of-absorbing-it/.

Jones, Nicola, and Nature Magazine. "A Historic Deal to Protect the High Seas Makes Researchers 'Ecstatic.'" *Scientific American*. March 8, 2023. www.scientificamerican.com/article/a-historic-deal-to-protect-the-high-seas-makes-researchers-ecstatic/.

Ross, Erin, and Nature Magazine. "Amazon Rainforest Was Shaped by an Ancient Hunger for Fruits and Nuts." *Scientific American*. March 3, 2017. www.scientificamerican.com/article/amazon-rainforest-was-shaped-by-an-ancient-hunger-for-fruits-and-nuts/.

Shailer, Daniel. "Which Lost Species May be Found Again? Huge Study Reveals Clues." *Scientific American*. January 17, 2024.

www.scientificamerican.com/article/which-lost-species-may-be-found-again-huge-study-reveals-clues/.

Stierwalt, Sabrina. "The Mariana Trench is 7 Miles Deep: What's Down There?" *Scientific American*. May 29, 2020. www.scientificamerican.com/article/the-mariana-trench-is-7-miles-deep-whats-down-there/.

Witze, Alexandra, and Nature Magazine. "Chinese Expedition Reveals Unexplored Section of Mysterious Arctic Ocean Ridge." *Scientific American*. November 13, 2025. www.scientificamerican.com/article/chinese-expedition-reveals-unexplored-section-of-mysterious-arctic-ocean/.

CITATIONS

1.1 We've Only Seen 0.001 Percent of Earth's Seafloor. Here's What That Really Means by Gayoung Lee (May 9, 2025); 1.2 Mining the Deep Sea Could Threaten a Source of Ocean Oxygen by Rachel Feltman, Jeffery DelViscio & Alex Sugiura (August 27, 2025); 1.3 Stunning Antarctic Sea Creatures Discovered after Iceberg Breaks Away by Ashley Balzer Vigil (March 21, 2025); 1.4 Dive into a Vanishing Invisible Forest to See What Climate Has Changed by Dominic Smith & Andrew Robinson (July 20, 2022); 1.5 "Dark Oxygen" Discovered Coming from Mineral Deposits on Deep Seafloor by Allison Parshall (July 22, 2024); 1.6 Strange Ecosystem Found Thriving below Seafloor Hydrothermal Vents by Jack Tamisiea (August 9, 2023); 1.7 Ocean Discoveries Are Revising Long-Held Truths about Life by Timothy Shank (August 1, 2022); 1.8 Bizarro Life-Forms Inhabiting Deep-Sea Vents May Be at Risk by Shannon Hall (August 4, 2017); 1.9 Mysterious Galápagos Reefs Harbor Strawberry Squid and Other Fantastic Creatures by Jack Tamisiea (November 2, 2023); 1.10 Seals Show Scientists an Unknown Antarctic Canyon by Ethan Freedman 1.11 The Ocean's Wilderness Areas Are Smaller Than You Think—and They're Disappearing Fast by Kendall Jones & James Watson (December 1, 2018); 1.12 Four New Octopus Species Discovered in the Deep Sea by Ashley Balzer Vigil (January 16, 2024); 1.13 The Mystery of Milky Seas Is Finally Being Solved by Michelle Nijhuis (August 1, 2022); 1.14 Bizarre Ecosystem Discovered More Than Two Miles beneath Arctic Ocean by Claire Cameron (December 25, 2025); 1.15 See the Lush Kelp Forests Scientists Are Fighting for as Oceans Warm by Avery Schuyler Nunn (May 15, 2025); 1.16 Slide Show: Science in Depth–Mini Subs Unlock Mysteries Deep Below the Ocean's Surface by Emily Anthes (April 8, 2009); 2.1 Indigenous Lands Ace Biodiversity Measurements by Jason G. Goldman (August 9, 2021); 2.2 Indigenous Amazon Communities Fight Deforestation with New Early-Alert Tool by Annie Sneed (August 9, 2021); 2.3 Great Nicobar Island Is a Paradise in Danger by Madhusree Mukerjee 3.1 Arctic Exploitation May Harm Animals Large and Small by Chiara Eisner (March 5, 2020); 3.2 The Arctic Is in Dire Straits, 20 Years of Reporting Show by Andrea Thompson (December 16, 2025); 4.1 Out of Sight, 'Dark Fungi' Run the World from the Shadows by Cody Cottier (June 21, 2024); 4.2 Drones Sample Rare Specimens from Cliffs and Other Dangerous Places by Susan Cosier (October 12, 2022); 4.3 Under Soil and above Caves, a Warren of Hidden Life by Jennifer Frazer (May 3, 2016); 4.4 Volcano Erupts after Lying Dormant for 12,000 Years, Sending Scientists Scrambling by Stephanie Pappas (November 24, 2025); 4.5 Giant Volcano Rewrites the Story of Seafloor Formation by William W. Sager (May 1, 2020); 4.6 Meet the Magnificent Microbes of the Deep Unknown by Jeffery DelViscio (April 10, 2023); 4.7 Mangrove Trees Are on the Move, Taking the Tropics with Them by Michael Adno (June 25, 2024); 5.1 How Climate Change Is Leaving Some Species with "Nowhere Left to Go" by Fionna M. D. Samuel (July 5, 2022); 5.2 The Reason Antarctica Is Melting: Shifting Winds, Driven by Global Warming by Annie Sneed (August 16, 2019) 5.3 Humans Have Crossed 7 of 9 "Planetary Boundaries" by Andrea Thompson (October 3, 2025).

INDEX

A

Alliance for Zero Extinction, 79
anemones, 22, 48
Antarctic ice, 22–23, 147–149
Arctic biome, 100

B

biodiversity, 23, 39, 46, 52, 54, 74, 76, 79, 91, 104, 144, 150, 152
biogeographic boundaries, 40
bioluminescence, 58–65
biosphere, 79, 107
black rocks, 12–13
boreal forest biome, 100

C

chemical pollution, 94, 97, 150
chemosynthetic creatures, 67
climate change, 12, 16, 22, 26, 29, 69, 72, 74, 80, 82, 91, 132, 141, 143–144, 146–147, 151
copepods, 34, 59, 111, 113–114
coral diversity, 90
coral reefs, 39, 46–47, 51, 81–82, 87, 131, 143

D

dark fungi, 103–107
dark oxygen, 19, 31
deep sea, 8–13, 19, 29, 32, 34, 39, 54, 56, 65, 67, 72
deep-sea mining, 16–18, 20, 30–32, 36, 48, 65, 68
deforestation, 28, 76–77, 91
dolphins, 80, 82–83

E

ecosystems, 10, 22–23, 25, 28–29, 32, 34, 36, 38–39, 46–48, 52, 67–68, 76, 94, 100, 104–106, 111, 126, 132, 141, 150–151
environmental DNA (eDNA), 104–105, 107
environmental impact assessment (EIA), 80, 82, 85

F

Falkor (too), 22, 34, 46, 48, 118, 120
fishing, 51–52, 75, 82, 94–97

G

Galathea Bay, 79–80, 82, 91
genetic adaptations, 69

H

hydrothermal organisms, 38
hydrothermal vents, 10, 34–36, 38–39, 42, 44, 54–55, 67–68

I
icebergs, 22–23
ice shelf, 22–23
International Seabed Authority, 19, 32

K
kelp, 25–30, 69–70, 143

M
marine desert,18
marine life, 12, 52, 119
Meroe Island, 90
microbes, 15–16, 31–32, 36, 89, 125–129
milky seas, 58–63
minerals, 12–13, 15–17, 30, 36, 77, 112
monkeys, 83, 91

N
noise pollution, 97

O
ocean acidification, 142, 150–151
Ocean Discovery League, 8
ocean floor, 9–10, 12–13, 35, 49, 64–65, 68, 81
octopuses, 22, 34, 46, 54–55
otters, 27, 69

P
plate tectonics, 10, 127–128

R
rainforest, 79, 87, 89, 91, 103

S
sea ice, 94, 99–100
sea urchins, 26–29, 69
seawater electrolysis, 14, 31
SuBastian robot, 22, 47–48
submarine exploration, 11
submersible expeditions, 8, 63

T
Tamu Massif, 118–122

V
variations in biology, 44
visual imaging, 9
volcanoes, 13, 34, 46, 116–123, 127

W
whales, 13, 46, 80, 82–83, 94, 96–98, 143

Z
zooplankton, 94–95